Did you say FREE trade?

The Economic 'Partnership' Agreement
European Union - West Africa

Jacques Berthelot

Did you say FREE trade?

The Economic 'Partnership' Agreement European Union - West Africa

Prefaces of
Mamadou Cissokho and Ken Ukaoha

L'Harmattan

Of the same author

Les coopératives agricoles en économie concurrentielle,
Cujas, 1972

Les sillons de la faim, together with François de Ravignan,
L'Harmattan, 1980

L'agriculture, talon d'Achille de la mondialisation,
L'Harmattan, 2001

Réguler les prix agricoles,
L'Harmattan, 2013

Vous avez dit LIBRE échange ?
L'Accord de Partenariat économique
Union européenne-Afrique de l'Ouest
L'Harmattan, 2018

Translation by Jean Lucien Dibombe Tshamulamba

5-7, rue de l'Ecole-Polytechnique, 75005 Paris

http://www.editions-harmattan.fr

ISBN : 978-2-343-15840-2
EAN : 9782343158402

CONTENTS

PREFACE OF MAMADOU CISSOKHO

Honorary President of ROPPA
(Network of Farmers and Producers' Organisations of West Africa)[1]

The Yaoundé and Lomé agreements have not produced the desired results over several decades in terms of share of exports towards the European market, industrial development or good governance by the States, mainly because these agreements were implemented at the time of the establishment of young states, politically sovereign indeed, whilst the economic levers have remained in the hands of the colonising countries.

Moreover, reform attempts for a greater autonomy have been painfully achieved through Structural Adjustments: reimbursement of over-billed industrialisation projects, net losses in privatisation efforts, credit financing of education and health, loss of support for agro-silvo-pastoral activities creating resources and jobs in rural areas ... and all this in a context of deteriorating terms of trade of agricultural commodities.

It is from the year 2000 that the majority of the Sub-Saharan African countries have concluded the negotiations on the Structural Adjustment Program for Agriculture with the World Bank, while participating in the trade negotiations within the WTO. The group of 77 developing countries have then put the Doha Round on the WTO agenda, mainly to temper the inequities in agricultural

---

[1] Member of ECOWAS Task Forces on Ecowap (common agricultural policy) and on free circulation of goods, services and people; President of the network of civil society on ECOWAS development programme.

trade. However, the systematic opposition by developed countries, especially from the EU, refusing to admit the dumping effect of its domestic agricultural subsidies has blocked this process.

At least the Lomé Conventions established non-reciprocal trade agreements and the relationship with ACP countries depended on the Development and Cooperation DG (DEVCO) instead of the Trade DG, which has been involved in the EPA negotiations when its only concern is that of opening new markets for EU exports.

Two groups of countries are found in the economic integration regions of Africa: the vast majority called least developed countries (LDCs) are supposed to benefit from the EU's "Everything but Arms" regime, unlike the other, considered to be developing countries (DCs).

The Cotonou Agreement (2000 - 2020) facilitated the EPA negotiations, which actually took off in 2005 with the signing phase planned for 2007. It can be noted with satisfaction that the mobilisation of the civil society, parliamentarians and political parties from both ACP and EU countries, has made it possible to postpone the signing date deadline from 2007 to 2015. ECOWAS Heads of State proposed DPAs (Development Partnership Agreements), instead of EPAs, to promote the establishment of a single market.

The interest of the EPAs proposed by the EU does not take into account a number of factors:

- It is regrettable to note that EU funding is mainly focused on EPAs impact assessments: recruitment of experts, validation of reports and their dissemination... or non-dissemination if their impact is proved negative.
- As usual, ECOWAS negotiated more on financial support promises rather than on the negative impacts of the signing.

- In the framework of the implementation of the African Union's African Agriculture Development Program (CAADP), it has been shown that exports outside Africa are much more focused on raw agricultural produce, while intra-African trade is more on value-added processed products.
- The complex diversity and multiplicity of EU negotiations with impacts or linkages to EPAs does not facilitate a good understanding of the value and urgency of their signature. The EU does not care about the erosion of the competitiveness of ACP countries due to the multiplication of its free trade bilateral agreements with countries exporting the same products, agricultural produce in particular, whereas it should associate ACP countries to these agreements, let alone the bilateral investment agreements signed with its member States.
- Similarly, EPAs negotiation should have taken into account the increasingly important partnerships established by ACP countries with the United States (AGOA), China and India. The African Continental Free Trade Area (AfCFTA), largely supported by the EU, should have been negotiated with the Regional Economic Communities in order to consolidate the acquis of regional integration if the AfCFTA is to succeed in the future.

I think it is to avoid all these pitfalls that Nigeria wisely decided not to align itself, thus providing ECOWAS with the opportunity to adjust its positions.

Yes, as I said and wrote it, EPAs are Economic Poverty Agreements.

I salute Jacques for his efforts in monitoring the risks in signing and implementing EPAs and, especially, for supporting farmers' organisations and their partner NGOs.

PREFACE OF KEN UKAOHA

President of NANTS
(National Association of Nigerian Traders)[2]

The revised Cotonou Agreement of 2010 categorically underlines the fundamental principle of "*equality of partners and ownership of development strategies: in order to achieve the objectives of the partnership, the ACP States determine, in sovereignty, the development strategies of their economies and societies... EU development partners align their programs with these strategies*".

It is therefore difficult to understand the EU pressures on Nigeria to sign the West Africa (WA) EPA. President Mohammadu Buhari was very emphatic in his speech of February 3, 2016 to the European Parliament, when he asserted that: "*Nigeria expresses its reservations because signing on to EPA in its current form will negate its industrial revolution plan. The industrialisation plan aims at moving the country from being an importer of most products to an industrial nation that can at least meet its national needs. Nigeria also believes that the agreement will undermine the regional economic integration since it has already created three different trade regimes in West Africa*".

Despite continued pressure on Nigeria to sign the West African EPA, our President reiterated (April 9, 2018) to the new EU Ambassador that Nigeria's stance on the EPA

---

[2] Ken UKAOHA, Esq, is a foremost Trade Lawyer; Expert in Negotiations and Advocacy; Member of ECOWAS Task Force on Trade, and the President of NANTS.

has not changed as it would jeopardise the creation of millions of jobs for a youth who would otherwise be deprived of a future.

Furthermore, by ratifying the interim EPAs (iEPAs) of Côte d'Ivoire (CI) and Ghana, which have been implemented since the end of 2016 and will become permanent in the absence of the regional EPA, what the EU will have achieved is the final destruction of the progressive regional integration process at work since the Treaty of Lagos (1975) creating the ECOWAS.

The said regional integration objective will be even more destroyed by the two iEPAs of CI and Ghana that their Most Favoured Nation (MFN) clause forces them to grant to the EU the same market access of 90% of imports they have agreed to grant to all African countries when they signed the agreement on the African Continental Free Trade Area (AfCFTA) on 21 March in Kigali, instead of 75% in the iEPAs texts. Nigeria refused to sign this agreement as being much premature and devised in a top-down manner whereas it could be justified only once the regional integration of each Regional Economic Community (REC) is much more advanced. Nevertheless, once more, the EU Commission greeted the AfCFTA and committed to continue to support its implementation.

In that context Jacques Berthelot's analysis of the multiple manoeuvres and untruths used by the European Commission to impose the WA-EPA and the iEPAs is welcome.

I still personally believe that the soft-landing approach is for parties to eschew their ego and get back to the negotiation table with a view to re-negotiating some of the thematic issues that stand as stumbling blocks to the agreement. An appreciable level of understanding, willingness and commitment to possible trade-offs is imperative and needful in order to achieve a win-win outcome. Let us hope that parties to the agreement, especially the EU, will recognise the importance of pursuing the same path as a good basis for fashioning a mutually beneficial future of EU-WA relations, particularly within the context of post-Cotonou era.

What you get by dishonesty you may enjoy like the finest food, but sooner or later it will be like a mouthful of sand

Salomon's Proverbs, 20-17

INTRODUCTION

The history of the Economic Partnership Agreements (EPAs) between the European Union (EU) and the ACP (Africa, Caribbean and Pacific) countries – all former colonies of France, United Kingdom (UK), Portugal, Italy, Spain, with the exception of Liberia – illustrates the fact that their access to political independence since 1960 has remained formal, the EU having done everything possible to impose Economic Partnership Agreements (EPAs) which are rather economic impoverishment agreements.

These ACP States, including those of sub-Saharan Africa (SSA), of which West Africa (WA) – covering the 15 States of ECOWAS (Economic Community of West African States) plus Mauritania – and the East African Community (EAC), have been misled by European institutions (the Commission, the Council and the Parliament) to sign, provisionally apply, then ratify and implement regional or interim EPAs (iEPAs), among which those of Côte d'Ivoire (CI) and Ghana, on the basis of untruths from the European Commission (EC) General Directorate (DG) of Trade. It is not too late to denounce these tainted EPAs on the eve of the renegotiation of the Cotonou Agreement, which expires in 2020 so as to govern future relations between the EU and ACP countries. Needless to point out that those relations will be established without the United Kingdom (UK) since Brexit is expected to be effective on March 29, 2019.

On April 9, 2018, President Muhammadu Buhari of Nigeria told the new EU ambassador, when he came to present him his credentials, that his country was determined not to sign the WA-EPA, reiterating his speech of February 3, 2016 to the European Parliament, because that would jeopardise the industrialisation of the country and impede the creation of millions of jobs for a youth that, otherwise, would be deprived of a future. However, the EU has always recognised that the WA-EPA could not be finalised without Nigeria, which accounted in 2016 for 72% of the WA's GDP and 52% of its population.

The EU and ECOWAS have now their back against the wall, particularly CI and Ghana, which have signed towards the end of 2007 interim EPAs (iEPAs), and implemented them since the end of 2016 in the hope that the WA-EPA will be finalised so as to keep the entry at zero customs duty for their exports to the EU market.

Without a regional EPA, the iEPAs of CI and Ghana will become permanent and thus torpedo the slow process of regional integration at work since the creation of ECOWAS in 1975, whereas the primary objective of the EPAs and the Cotonou Agreement of 2000 between the EU and the ACP (Africa-Caribbean-Pacific) countries is to promote regional integration in the Regional Economic Communities (RECs) of the ACP countries, of which ECOWAS. Indeed, while the iEPAs will liberalise, that is to say gradually eliminate their customs duties on their imports from the EU over 15 years, from 3 September 2018 for CI and 15 December 2021 for Ghana, the other WA States will be forced to tax their imports from these two countries. Otherwise they will be over-flooded with the products that CI and Ghana will import duty free from the EU and, more generally, with the finished products they will have manufactured from EU inputs and capital goods accounting for 80% of their imports from the EU.

However, this observation will become much more complex insofar as only 13 out of the 16 WA States, of which CI and Ghana, have signed the agreement on the African Continental Free Trade Area (AfCFTA) on 21

March 2018, during the extraordinary Summit of Heads of State and Government of the African Union[3], but Nigeria, Benin and Guinea Bissau have not signed them up to now. Yet, this agreement commits the 13 WA States to remove their tariffs on 90% of their imports from Africa, and the clause of the Most Favoured Nation (MFN) registered in the APEi of Côte d'Ivoire and Ghana obliges them to grant the same benefits to the EU. This will imply much higher customs revenue losses than the already considerable losses calculated for their iEPAs of which liberalisation should cover 75% of imports from the EU.

In this context it is useful to analyse all the manoeuvres and untruths used by the EU DG Trade to impose the WA-EPA and the iEPAs of CI and Ghana, knowing that its behaviour has been very similar in imposing the EPAs on the other ACP countries.

---

[3] *The folly of the Africa's Continental Free Trade Area (AfCFTA)*, SOL, September 4, 2017, https://www.sol-asso.fr/wp-content/uploads/2017/10/The-folly-of-the-Africas-Continental-Free-Trade-Area-September-4-2017.pdf

I - THE EPAS WOULD HAVE BEEN IMPOSED BY THE WTO RULES

1.1 - WTO authorises trade preferences according to the level of development

The widely shared argument that it was legally impossible to maintain the non-reciprocal trade preferences of the Lomé Agreements between the EU and the ACP countries does not hold. The EC claimed that they were no longer WTO-compatible, especially after the EU was twice convicted of violating the GATT's non-discrimination principle following complaints from the 9 Latin American banana exporting countries – 3 Andean countries (Colombia, Ecuador, Peru) and 6 non-ACP Central American countries (Costa Rica, Guatemala, Honduras, Nicaragua, Panama, El Salvador) – as they had to pay customs duties (CDs) to the EU while the ACP countries were exempted.

Yet, if discrimination is prohibited by the GATT and the WTO according to a geographical criterion, it is possible according to the level of development. This has been at the origin of the EU's 'Generalised System of Preferences' (GSP) since 1971 for developing countries (DCs) –which benefit from lower ad valorem customs duties (CDs) of about 30% than on the 'Most Favoured Nation' (MFN) regime applied to developed countries – and duty free-quota free (DFQF) for the 'Least Developed Countries' (LDCs) since the EU 'Everything But Arms' (EBA) Decision of 2001. Hence the GSP+ status which exempts most of the exports to the EU from customs duties, except for some products subject to the MFN Customs Law applied to countries without trade preferences, which comply with criteria of economic vulnerability and implement 27 international conventions on human and social rights, environmental protection and good governance.

In the India's WTO case in 2012 against the EU's GSP preferential drug scheme (precursor of the GSP+), the Appellate Body concluded in 2014 that "*if a developed Member country granted additional tariff preferences under its GSP scheme to respond positively to the widely recognised 'development, financial and trade needs' of developing countries within the meaning of paragraph 3 (c) of the Enabling Clause that 'positive response' would not, as such, be inconsistent with the 'non-discriminatory' requirement in footnote 3 of the Enabling Clause, even if those requirements were not common to all developing countries or shared by them all*"[4].

Yet, the per capita GDP of the nine Latin American countries was 2.3 times higher in 1995 than that of the three banana exporting African countries (Cameroon, CI and Ghana) and was 3.9 times higher in 2016 ($ 5,557 vs. $ 1,433). Even India should not oppose it since its 2016 per capita GDP is 20% higher than that of these three countries and, under its LDC regime created in 2008 and revised in 2014, 98.2% of its imports (as a percentage of tariff lines) from LDCs, including 34 from ACP countries, are duty free[5]. And the per capita GDP of the EU28 ($

[4] *European Communities — Conditions for the Granting of Tariff Preferences to Developing Countries*, Appellate Body, 7 April 2004 https://www.wto.org/english/tratop_e/dispu_e/cases_e/ds246_e.htm

[5] https://www.un.org/ldcportal/preferential-market-access-indias-duty-free-tariff-preference-scheme-for-ldcs/

31,785) was 20.8 times higher in 2017 than that of WA ($ 1,527).

The EU could all the more obtain a new waiver from the WTO to maintain its non-reciprocal preferences now that the "banana war" was buried twice. First, by the December 2009 agreement at the WTO where Latin American countries have agreed that the EU could maintain its duty- free imports from ACP countries in return for a reduction of the CDs on their exports from € 148 per tonne (€/t) in 2010 to 114 €/t in 2017[6]. Then by the Free Trade Agreements (FTAs) concluded with these countries in 2012 [7] (in 2015 for Ecuador) which programmed a stronger reduction of their CDs, falling to 75 €/t from 2020 against the normal MFN duty of 127 €/t (reduced to 117 €/t since 1 January 2018) and the abolition of import quotas.

If the EU had buried this war as early as 2000, it could have obtained a waiver from the WTO to extend the Lomé preferential agreements, especially for SSA countries, as was the case for the United States (US) for the AGOA (African Growth Opportunity Act) also in May 2000, with a renewed exemption for 10 years in 2015 [8] with the unanimous consensus of the WTO, including that of the EU[9]. Furthermore AGOA does not hesitate to "*Address*

---

6 http://ictsd.org/i/trade-and-sustainable-development-agenda/103018/#respond

7 http://agritrade.cta.int/fr/Agriculture/Produits-de-base/Banane/Les-exportations-de-bananes-de-l-Amerique-centrale-et-du-Sud-vers-l-UE-boostees-par-les-accords-de-libre-echange-malgre-une-performance-variable

8 https://agoa.info/images/documents/5659/agoa-extension-and-enhancement-act-of-2015-2.pdf

9 HTTP://EUR-LEX.EUROPA.EU/LEGAL-CONTENT/EN/ALL/?URI=COM%3A2015%3A0464%3AFIN

unfair practices by the European Union that conditions African access to the European market on signing imbalanced and substandard trade agreements" [10]. However, it is not too late to ask for this waiver, especially in the framework of the reflections on the agreement that will succeed Cotonou, which expires in 2020.

1.2 - **<u>The EU has reneged on its "Everything But Arms" Decision and contradicted the WTO stance on LDCs</u>**

It is the EU that has defined the geopolitical scope of the SSA's 5 regional EPAs, often in contradiction with the perimeters of the Regional Economic Communities (RECs)[11], ensuring that each included LDCs and non-LDCs (also called developing countries, DCs). By requiring that all the member States of each regional EPA abolish their CDs on about 80% of EU exports, this was cancelling the preferences of its 2001 'Everything But Arms' (EBA) Decision recognising non reciprocal DFQF access for LDCs which could tax EU exports. And this on the pretext of promoting the regional integration of each

---

[10] https://agoa.info/images/documents/5659/agoa-extension-and-enhancement-act-of-2015-2.pdf

[11] The West African (WA) EPA includes ECOWAS (Economic Community of West African States, 15 States) plus Mauritania; the Central Africa EPA comprises CEMAC (Economic Community of Central African States, 6 States) plus the Democratic Republic of Congo (DRC) and Sao Tome and Principe; the EAC EPA (East African Economic Community, 5 States); the Southern Africa Development Community (SADC) EPA comprises only 6 out of 15 States; the ESA EPA (from Eastern and Southern Africa) includes only 4 of the 16 COMESA States. And many States belong to several RECs, hence the name "spaghettis' bowl" for these multiple affiliations.

regional EPA which would not work with different trade regimes since the free movement of products would oblige the LDCs to tax imports from the DCs to avoid being invaded by products that they would import duty free from the EU.

Yet a legal solution compatible with EBA and the WTO rules would have been to deduct from the percentage to be liberalised in each regional EPA that of exports from the EU to the LDCs. For the WA-EPA, 43.5% of EU exports to the 13 LDCs in 2015 would have been deducted from the 76.2% to be liberalised, which would fall to 32.7%; and for the EAC-EPA, 45.4% of exports to the 4 LDCs in 2015 would have been deducted from the 82.6% to be liberalised, which would fall to 37.2%.

However, the EU has rejected this legal interpretation, which is too much of a hindrance to its trade objectives. Yet the House of Commons International Development Committee had defended this possibility on April 6, 2005: "*We do not think things should be complicated for the LDCs. The EBA should be a real option for LDCs. And they should not have to offer reciprocal market access to the EU until they have graduated from LDC status. The EBA should not conflict with regional integration initiatives in the ACP, especially given the emphasis that DG Trade is placing on the importance of regional integration*"[12].

Indeed, during the debate, the EU Trade Commissioner Peter Mandelson said: "*ACP countries will be no worse off*

---

[12] House of Commons International Development Committee, *Fair trade? The European Union's trade agreements with African, Caribbean and Pacific countries*, 6 April 2005, https://publications.parliament.uk/pa/cm200405/cmselect/cmintdev/68/68.pdf.

joining once the EPAs kick in, from the EBA. That is very important. We are asking for 'EBA plus', not 'EBA minus'". And the drafter of the House of Commons concluded: "*We understand 'EBA plus' to mean that LDCs who choose to sign an EPA will not have to offer the EU reciprocal market access*".

It may be objected that, even with an opening rate of 32.7% for WA and 37.2% for EAC, it would still be necessary for LDCs to tax imports from non-LDCs. In fact, no, because the problem would be easily solved since the duty-free tariff lines (TLs) represent precisely 37.4% of the 5,274 TLs of the EAC[13], so that the entire EAC would have nothing to liberalise. And, although only 85 TLs of WA are duty-free, 2,146 TLs, or 36.4% of the total 5,899 TLs, are taxed at 5% and would therefore be at zero CD in the first year of liberalisation, in T5[14].

1.3 - <u>The EU's priority is to open all-round markets</u>

The EU did not want to renew non-reciprocal agreements with ACP countries as it pursues an all-out market access strategy by multiplying its FTAs with most developed and emerging countries in order to increase its exports while guaranteeing its supply of raw materials at world prices. An expanded strategy since the standstill of the Doha Round negotiations at the WTO and clearly stated in the October 2006 'Global Europe'[15] documents by Commissioner for Trade Peter Mandelson and 'Trade for All'[16] of Commissioner Cecilia Malström in June 2015.

---

[13] https://www.theigc.org/wp-content/uploads/2017/11/Sheperd-et-al-2017-policy-paper1.pdf

[14] https://www.wto.org/english/tratop_e/tpr_e/s362-00_e.pdf

[15] http://trade.ec.europa.eu/doclib/docs/2006/october/tradoc_130376.pdf

[16] http://trade.ec.europa.eu/doclib/docs/2015/october/tradoc_153846.pdf

This is why the EPAs were negotiated and managed by DG Trade, while the Lomé Conventions were managed by the DG Cooperation and Development (DEVCO).

Another evidence of the priority given to market access in ACP countries stems from the change in Article 37 in the 2010 revision of the Cotonou Agreement, which was originally drafted in 2000 in paragraphs 5 and 6 of the same Agreement: "*5. Negotiations of the economic partnership agreements will be undertaken with ACP countries which consider themselves in a position to do so, at the level they consider appropriate and in accordance with the procedures agreed by the ACP Group, taking into account regional integration process within the ACP. 6. In 2004, the Community will assess the situation of the non-LDC which, after consultations with the Community decide that they are not in a position to enter into economic partnership agreements and will examine all alternative possibilities, in order to provide these countries with a new framework for trade which is equivalent to their existing situation and in conformity with WTO rules*"[17].

However, while this provision was confirmed in the 2005 revision, only paragraph 5 (now 3) of Article 37 remained, slightly modified, in the 2010 revision: "*Negotiations of the Economic Partnership Agreements will be pursued with ACP countries which consider themselves in a position to do so, at the level they consider appropriate and in accordance with the procedures agreed by the ACP Group, and with a view to supporting regional integration process within the ACP*", but paragraph 6 on alternatives to EPAs disappeared. Paragraph 7 of the new Article 37 only states that "*Once ACP States have concluded an Economic*

[17] http://eur-lex.europa.eu/legal-content/EN/TXT/?uri=celex:22000A1215(01)

Partnership Agreement, those ACP States which are not Parties to such Agreement can seek accession at any time", without possible alternatives to EPAs.

1.4 – **DG Trade refused to amend the already initialed EPAs**

Moreover, DG Trade has systematically refused to discuss possible amendments to the already initialed EPA texts to allow some reluctant States to sign them. This is first the case of Nigeria whose firm position not to sign the regional WA-EPA as it stands was solemnly expressed by President Muhammadu Buhari before the plenary session of the European Parliament on 3 February 2016 in Strasbourg[18] because it would considerably undermine his industrialisation agenda. Despite the multiple pressures exerted on Nigeria by the European Commission, some EU member States, other ECOWAS States (except The Gambia) and European firms, President Buhari confirmed on April 9, 2018 to the new EU Ambassador that his stance did not change.

During the debate of 13 October 2016 of the European Parliament's International Commission (INTA) on the ratification of the Ghana Interim EPA (iEPA), the Minister of Foreign Affairs, Ms. Hannah Tetteh[19], underlined clearly that there was no question of renegotiating the regional EPA concluded and initialed by all Members on 10 July 2014, the only thing preventing its implementation

[18] http://www.nta.ng/2016/02/03/president-buhari-assures-eu-of-nigerias-commitment-to-protection-of-human-rights-calls-for-mutually-beneficial-economic-relations-with-europe/

[19] http://www.europarl.europa.eu/news/en/news-room/20161005IPR45679/committee-on-international-trade-meeting-13102016-(am)

being the deadline requested by Nigeria to better analyse its provisions before signing. The Head of EPAs Division at DG Trade, Sandra Gallina, confirmed the position of the Minister that the Commission is not ready to renegotiate the regional EPA.

DG Trade opposed the same refusal to Tanzania's request to renegotiate the EAC-EPA to allow it to sign, as well as to the request of the five CEMAC States other than Cameroon to allow them to sign the Central African EPA that Cameroon has signed, ratified and implemented[20] since August 4, 2014: "*As indicated in our letter of July 19, our services are at your disposal to study with you the terms and conditions of this agreement. accession to the current interim agreement between the EU and Cameroon, and we wish to reiterate that it cannot therefore be a question of relaunching the regional negotiations which were interrupted in 2011 and in particular to discuss the text of a new agreement*"[21].

---

[20] The terminology of the stages of implementation of international trade treaties is complex: the first is the "initialing" of the treaty by the official negotiators (senior officials) who confirm its content – which was done for the WA EPA on June 30, 2014 in Ouagadougou –, the second the "confirmation of the initialing", that is to say, the intention to finalise the treaty, by the Heads of State – what was done for the WA EPA on July 10, 2014 in Abuja –, the third the formal signature by all the Heads of State – what was done for the WA EPA on December 12, 2014 by the EU Foreign Affairs Council but 2 WA States AO (Nigeria, and Mauritania) have still not done so, with Nigeria's signature being obviously essential, and this signature is enough for the European Commission to decide on the "provisional application" of the treaty. But the official "implementation" requires "ratification" which, for the WA EPA, must be done by all EU parliaments and two-thirds of those of WA.

[21] https://www.237online.com/article-55428-l-ue-rompt-les-negociations-sur-un-apc-regional.html

Despite a new request from the President of the CEMAC Commission to DG Trade on March 15, 2018, the latter maintained that the EPA already implemented by Cameroon was not renegotiable[22].

As for the European Parliament, its position has always been that, since almost all the ACP States, notably those from WA, have initialed the EPAs, even if they have not signed it yet, it does not see how it could oppose it. The civil society protests from both the EU and ACP countries have failed to gather momentum because of the very little mobilisation against the EPAs, more focus being given to the protests against the EU-US TAFTA and the EU-Canada CETA. As regards the West African side, the failure was due to the fact that the Heads of State did not want to consult the civil society.

They preferred to yield to the sirens of the European lobbies and their local branches, particularly the French agribusiness firms. These include Robert Fabre's Compagnie Fruitière, which produces and exports most of the bananas and pineapples of CI, Ghana and Cameroon; the Mimran Group which owned the Grands Moulins of Abidjan and Dakar and the Compagnie Sucrière of Senegal, but has just sold them to a Moroccan group; the Thai Union Europe and notably MW Brands in Paris, which controls the bulk of CI's canned tuna exports to the EU, the Paul Paulet cannery in Douarnenez (France) under the "Petit Navire" brand (I noticed at the end of November 2017 that all canned tuna sold in the supermarkets of Abidjan were of various French brands); and the Bolloré Group which controls the Gulf of Guinea port infrastructure and participates in the export of products to the EU, including cocoa.

---

[22] https://www.bilaterals.org/?apres-son-retrait-en-2017-l-union

1.5 – **DG Trade has been deaf to official criticism from some EU States**

In addition to the many criticisms of EU and ACP solidarity NGOs, official criticism from some EU Member States has failed to counter the commercial aggression of DG Trade in imposing EPAs.

The United Kingdom (UK) Secretary of Commerce and Industry, Patricia Hewitt, raised concerns about EPAs on 22 March 2005: "*EPAs must be designed to deliver long-term development, economic growth and poverty reduction in ACP countries. We believe that in its work on EPAs with ACP regional groups, the EU should take a non-mercantilist approach and not pursue any offensive interests. Developing countries can benefit from liberalisation in the long run, provided they have the economic capacity and infrastructure they need to trade competitively... Each ACP regional group should make its own decisions on the timing, pace, sequencing, and product coverage of market opening in line with individual countries' national development plans and poverty reduction strategies... We will not force trade liberalisation on developing countries either through trade negotiations or aid conditionality... There should be an effective safeguard mechanism for ACP countries to use if faced with a surge of subsidised EU imports*"[23].

Unfortunately, the UK Trade White Paper of January 2018 about Brexit states the following: "*On EPAs, we have taken into account our partners' wishes for continuity and will seek to replicate the effects of these agreements as the UK leaves the EU. Our approach also takes into consideration the long-term benefits offered by*

---

23 http://webarchive.nationalarchives.gov.uk/20090609014244/http://www.berr.gov.uk/files/file9845.pdf

EPAs, recognising the need for more mature bilateral partnerships as countries move towards middle-income status and providing a strong continuity message to business"[24].

The delegation of the French National Assembly for the European Union unanimously adopted the long report on the EPAs by Jean-Claude Lefort on July 5, 2006, with the following conclusions (among others): 1. "*The delegation is seriously concerned by the fact that the implementation of free trade, despite the precautions currently envisaged by the European Commission, will result in a fiscal, agricultural, industrial and balance of payments shock of such a magnitude for our partners that it could jeopardise the achievement of the Millennium Development Goals, while sub-Saharan Africa suffers from delays so worrying that they pose a threat to international peace and stability; 2. The delegation thinks that if negotiations continued in the same way, the European Union would make a strategic, political, economic and social mistake with regard to the ACP countries, which will result in the disintegration of a relationship that is essential to the construction of a safer and more just world and to the reputation as well as the weight of European influence*"[25].

Commenting on her report of 15 June 2008 on EPAs to the French President Nicolas Sarkosy, Christiane Taubira summed up her conclusions in an interview of 7 July 2008 in the Journal du Dimanche: "*The EPAs are trade agreements and not development agreements. The Commission agrees. However, I do not think that free trade can lead to development. There is no example of*

24

https://www.gov.uk/government/uploads/system/uploads/attachment_data/file/671953/Trade_White_Paper_response_FINAL.pdf

25 http://www.assemblee-nationale.fr/12/europe/rap-info/i3251.asp

opening one's market that has led to development. The EPAs will remove all protections. By completely opening the markets, not only are the protections suppressed but the States are also disarmed, deprived of revenues, budgetary possibilities and intervention in the economy... It is no longer a matter of unlocking aid envelopes. The World Bank and the IMF are still unlocking envelopes and have been doing so for 25 years, getting the southern countries down to their knees with their structural adjustment policies and giving them emergency aids today. We should stop must taking people for granted. People are starving!"[26]

Unfortunately, like the UK, the French National Assembly approved on 25 June 2015 the ratification of CI's iEPA, based on political positions not supported by in-depth analyses[27].

As for Germany, Günter Nooke, Commissioner for Africa of the German Chancellor Angela Merkel, "*has severely criticised the EU's free trade agreement with several African countries, saying the EPA is undermining the development policy of Europe*"[28].

On March 19, 2012 the former Governor of the Central Bank of Nigeria, Professor Chukhuma Soludo, warned that signing EPAs would lead Africa to a '*second slavery*'[29].

---

[26] Christiane Taubira, "*Les gens crèvent de faim*", 7 Juliet 2008, http://www.abcburkina.net/fr/nos-dossiers/les-ape/637-taubira-les-gens-crevent-de-faim

[27] http://www.assemblee-nationale.fr/14/rapports/r2889.asp#P185_44359

[28] https://www.euractiv.com/section/development-policy/news/eu-africa-free-trade-agreement-destroys-development-policy-says-merkel-advisor/

[29] https://www.vanguardngr.com/2016/11/eus-epa-strategy-detrimental-africa-ecowas-farmers/

Ghana's President, Nana Akufo-Addo, told President Macron on December 30, 2017 during his visit to Accra after the EU-African Union Summit in Abidjan: "*We can no longer pursue a policy for our countries and regions that is based on the support given by the West, France or the European Union. This has not worked and it will not work*"[30].

The conference of the International Confederation of Trade Unions (ITUC) held in Lomé on 9 and 10 October 2017 concluded that "*The current EPA negotiations should stop; signed EPAs should not enter into force in their current form; and interim EPAs should be repealed*"[31].

---

[30] https://www.euractiv.com/section/development-policy/news/ghanas-president-surprised-macron-with-a-clear-rejection-of-development-aid/

[31] https://www.bilaterals.org/?outcomes-of-the-trade-union&lang=en

II – THE INTERIM EPAS OF CÔTE D'IVOIRE AND GHANA TORPEDO THE PRIMARY GOAL OF REGIONAL INTEGRATION IN WEST AFRICA

Like the Cotonou Agreement, the preamble and the first articles of the regional EPAs have multiplied the references to the first objective of strengthening their regional integration. For the WA-EPA in particular Article 4 states: "*1. The Parties recognise that regional integration is an essential part of their partnership and a powerful tool for achieving the objectives of this Agreement and agree to give it their strong support. 2. For the purposes referred to in paragraph 1 of this Article, the European Union Party shall contribute, according to the provisions of Part III of this Agreement, through technical and financial assistance to the efforts of the region with regard to integration, in particular the achievement of customs union and a common market*"[32].

2.1 - The European Commission pretends to believe that Nigeria will eventually sign the EPA

Yet the EU institutions – Commission, Council and Parliament – accepted by the end of 2007 the signing of interim EPAs (iEPAs) with some non-LDC developing

[32] http://data.consilium.europa.eu/doc/document/ST-13370-2014-INIT/en/pdf

countries, of which CI [33] and Ghana[34]. The preamble to CI iEPA states: "*PENDING the signing of a comprehensive Economic Partnership Agreement between West Africa and the European Union with a view to ensuring he sustained and harmonious development and integration of the West African Region; REAFFIRMING their commitment to supporting the regional integration process in West Africa, and in particular to promoting regional economic integration as an essential instrument for its integration in the world economy by helping the region to meet globalisation challenges and achieve its economic and social development objectives*". The preamble to Ghana's iEPA is similar.

The last official and grounded position of Nigeria is expressed in its report of 17 October 2017 to the WTO: "*Nigeria values and accords the highest premium to its economic and trading relationship with the European Union (EU) and all its individual member States. However, Nigeria has communicated to the EU that it shall neither sign nor ratify the ECOWAS European Union Economic Partnership Agreement (the EPA), in its present form. In this circumstance, appropriate measures including rules of origin are required in the implementation of ECOWAS CET in order to eliminate trade diversion and or trade deflection. Nigeria is in conversation with the EU at several levels, with the European Commission and several of its individual member States. Nigeria remains in contact and is in exploratory contacts at several levels*"[35]. In June 2017,

[33] http://eur-lex.europa.eu/legal-content/EN/TXT/?uri=CELEX:22009A0303%2801%29
[34] http://eur-lex.europa.eu/legal-content/EN/TXT/?uri=uriserv:OJ.L_.2016.287.01.0003.01.ENG
[35] https://www.wto.org/english/tratop_e/tpr_e/g356_e.pdf

during the debate on Nigeria's Trade Policy Review, on Turkey's request to clarify its positions on the EPA, the representative of Nigeria elaborated on the 10 grievances made to the EPA which would hinder its development objectives[36].

President Buhari very explicitly confirmed on 9 April 2018 to the new EU ambassador to Nigeria, Ketil Iversen Karlsen, who came to present him his credentials, that "*Nigeria refused to sign the EPA with the other ECOWAS countries because it needs to protect its economy, especially its industries and the small businesses that currently provide jobs for most Nigerians, including its youth*"[37]. He only repeated what he had already solemnly declared on 3 February 2016 at the Plenary Assembly of the European Parliament in Strasbourg.

Despite Nigeria's strong position and the EU Commission's refusal to change the text of the WA EPA, the European Parliament ratified Ghana's iEPA on 30 November 2016 and it has been implemented on 15 December 2016. It had also ratified CI's iEPA as of 25 March 2009 but the Ivorian Parliament only ratified it on 12 August 2016 and it has entered into force and been implemented on 3 September 2016[38].

---

[36] https://www.wto.org/french/tratop_f/tpr_f/tp456_f.htm

[37] https://www.thisdaylive.com/index.php/2018/04/10/buhari-l-declined-signing-regional-economic-pact-to-protect-local-industries-youths-fg-au-to-resume-afcfta/

[38] *L'absurde APE intérimaire de Côte d'Ivoire*, SOL, 31 mars 2018, https://www.sol-asso.fr/wp-content/uploads/2017/01/Labsurde-APE-int%C3%A9rimaire-de-C%C3%B4te-dIvoire-SOL-31-mars-2018.pdf

2.2 – The underlying differences in tariffs between the Côte d'Ivoire and Ghana iEPAs and the ECOWAS CET

The European Commission has continued to resolutely believe that Nigeria will eventually falter and that the regional EPA will be finalised. Meanwhile, CI and Ghana continued to apply the ECOWAS CET (Common External Tariff) theoretically in force since 1 January 2015 – even though it is not yet fully operational in all States – and not the CDs of their iEPAs, as confirmed by the EU Commission document written towards the end of 2016: "*Non-liberalized goods in the interim EPA: Côte d'Ivoire has excluded a number of agricultural products and non-agricultural processed products from liberalisation. This is essentially to protect agricultural markets and sensitive industries, but also to maintain tax revenues. For example, frozen chicken and other meats, onions, sugar, tobacco, beer, some cements and most textiles are excluded from liberalisation, and upon entry into the Ivorian market these imports will continue to be taxed at the normal rate (the ECOWAS Common External Tariff)*"[39].

Yet the current use of the WA CET instead of the iEPA CDs applied since the 3 September 2016 contradicts the standstill clause in Article 15 of the iEPA: "*No new customs duties on imports shall be introduced in trade between the Parties, nor shall those currently applied in trade between the Parties be increased from the date of entry into force of this Agreement. Notwithstanding paragraph 1, and as part of the finalisation of the common external tariff of the Economic Community Of West African States (ECOWAS), Côte d'Ivoire may until 31*

[39] http://trade.ec.europa.eu/doclib/docs/2017/february/tradoc_155315.pdf

December 2011 revise its basic customs duties on goods originating from the European Community insofar as the general impact of these duties is no higher than that resulting from the duties specified in Annex 2".

And what will happen from the beginning of the liberalisation of the iEPAs, knowing that: 1) the liberalisation schedules of the CDs of the 2 iEPAs are different; (2) all the Ghana iEPA tariff lines (TLs) or codes are of 6 digits (SH6) as opposed to 10 digits for CI iEPA and WA EPA; 3) the CDs are different for many products as well as their levels at the start and at the end of liberalisation; 4) some products with low CDs (5% or 10%) will be excluded from liberalization in the CI iEPA. Let's illustrate these points with some examples.

2.2.1 - Differences in liberalisation schedules

The first observation is that there is a contradiction in the timing of liberalisation displayed in Annex 2 of the CI's iEPA between the announcement "*For Group A Products, liberalisation extends from 1 January 2008 to 31 December 2012, i.e. over a period of five years*", and the long liberalisation table of TLs that follows, where we see that some TLs are liberalised as early as 1.5 years after the start of provisional implementation for certain products, hence from 3 February 2017.

Whereas, with the ECOWAS CET, all group A products – other than those with zero CD that remain at zero with the iEPA – are liberalised in T5 only, with the iEPA the losses of CDs – calculated at the EU28-UK FOB[40] value – should have started on 3 February 2017

[40] FOB (free on board): price of a product at the place (port, airport, station) of an exporting country; CIF (costs, insurance, freight): price

(T1) for € 46,272. They will already be significant on 3 September 2018 (T2), at € 3,610 million (€ M), then will be very important in T3 (€ 30.4 M, or 62.1% of Group A losses) and T4 (€ 62.7 M, or 78.5% of group A losses).

Besides, these liberalised products from T1 to T4 are mainly inputs and capital goods that will reduce the cost of production of CI's finished products. Most capital goods, most often under Chapter 84 of the HS and taxed at 5%, will be liberalised in T3, which will greatly increase the competitiveness of CI products vis-à-vis that of other WA countries. This will affect in particular that of agricultural products, whose inputs, especially fertilisers, will be liberalised in T2 or T3, which should call into question their free movement without requiring a certificate of origin according to the current ECOWAS rules of origin.

A new contradiction emerges from the second meeting of the CI-EU EPA Committee of 21 and 22 March 2018 according to which "*The EU side has taken note of the tariff dismantling schedule presented by the Ivorian side and which provides for the start of tariff dismantling in January 2019*" [41] . Despite this change in the CI's dismantling schedule accepted by the representative of the European Commission in relation to the tariff offer ratified by the European Parliament and the UE Council, we will stick to the legal text providing that dismantling would have already begun on 3 February 2017 and would be significant as of 3 September 2018.

On the other hand, tariff dismantling will start in T5 only for Ghana's iEPA (on 15 December 2021), even if the initial EPA text of the end of December 2007 had

---

of a product arrived at the port, airport, station, of an importing country.

[41] http://trade.ec.europa.eu/doclib/docs/2018/march/tradoc_156659.pdf

provided that liberalisation for group A products taxed at 5% would be made in 5 annual phases starting in T1, which was then modified in 2008 by the total liberalisation of this group A in T5.

2.2.2 - All the Ghana iEPA tariff lines have 6 digits (HS6)

These TLs are therefore much less precise than the 10-digit TLs of the CI iEPA and WA EPA, which are identical except that, in the WA CET in force since 1 January 2015, many LTs in the fifth band of CDs are at 35%. For example, in Ghana iEPA, code 040210 (skimmed milk powder with less than 1.5% fat, with or without added sugar) and code 040229 (milk powder with more than 1.5% fat, with the addition of sugar) are taxed at 20% and will not be fully liberalised until T20, whereas in CI iEPA and in the WA EPA, the corresponding 10-digit codes are only taxed at 5% and will be liberalised in T5.

2.2.3 - The CDs are different for many products, as well as their levels at the start and at the end of liberalisation

No TL on cotton (Chapter 52) other than the unprocessed raw cotton (code 5201) is excluded from liberalisation in Ghana iEPA, while all TLs (other than raw cotton) are excluded in CI iEPA and WA EPA. Code 5208110000 (cotton fabrics, at least 85% cotton, unbleached, plain weave, weighing not more than 100 g/m2) which is taxed at 10% in CI will therefore be excluded from liberalisation while the code 520811 of Ghana, taxed at 20%, will be fully liberalized in T20.

All poultry meats are excluded from liberalisation in the Ghana iEPA as in the WA EPA, while the CI iEPA only excludes frozen meat and liberalises fresh or chilled meat, in T20 for chicken meat and in T15 for those of turkey, goose and duck.

The best example of the differences in CDs between the WA EPA and the CI and Ghana iEPAs as well as those of Eurostat is that of the CDs on fat-filled milk powder (FFMP). This skimmed milk powder (SMP) is re-fattened with palm oil (or coprah oil) and is also referred to as vegetable milk powder because these solid oils are cheaper than milk fat (butter or cream). Indeed the price of FFMP (represented supposedly by code 19019099) imported in WA from the EU in 2017 was 47.2% lower than the price of the whole milk powder.

Hence the explosion of exports of this type of FFMP to WA, which were presumably multiplied by 2.1 between 2010 and 2017 (from 123,407 tonnes to 258,424 tonnes), against a reduction of 53% for whole milk powder (from 61,769 tonnes to 32,905 tonnes). The use of 'supposedly' and 'presumably' is justified by the fact that the precise amount is not known due to lack of a unique identification code, which led Eurostat to ask the consulting firm GIRA to conduct a research and propose one. We only know that it lies in Eurostat sub-codes of code 190190 (probably 19019099) or code 2106, even if Paul Goodison uses the whole code 190190[42].

In the WA EPA, imports under the code 1901901000 – with the label "Preparations of milk containing vegetable fats and oils, powdered or granulated, in packages of 25 kg or more" – and the code 1091902000 – with the same label but for packages of 12.5 to 25 kg – are classified in group A of products liberalised in T5. On the other hand,

[42] http://epamonitoring.net/

imports under the code 19019099 are classified as 'others' in group D of the excluded products taxed at 20%. In addition, refined palm oil is taxed at 35% in category D of products excluded from liberalisation, regardless of the weight of packaging. But the main problem is that we do not have the data for WA imports under these codes but only those for EU exports for which the Eurostat codes are different.

For its part, CI iEPA provides for a 5% CD in Group C (liberalised after 13 years) for code 1901900010 – with the label "*Milk-based preparations containing vegetable fats in powder or granules packaged in packages of 25 kg or more*" –, bearing in mind that refined palm oil is taxed at 20% whether or not packaged for retail sale of a content not exceeding 5 litres. On the other hand, since Ghana has only 6-digit codes, all the products of code 190190 – which contains other products than re-fattened milk powder – are taxed at 10% in category B and the CD falls to 5% in T9 and to 0 in T10. Similarly, Ghana has only two 6-digit codes for palm oil which is also taxed at 10% in category D excluded from liberalisation.

While only the CDs at 5% (in group A) fall to 0 at the beginning of liberalisation (in T5) in the Ghana iEPA and WA EPA, in the CI iEPA a large number of TLs at 10% and even at 20% are classified also in group A and fall to 0 in T3, and sometimes even in T1 (3 September 2018). The losses of CDs of products taxed at 10% and 20% represent 80% of the losses of group A in the CI iEPA against 20% only for the products taxed at 5%. For example in the CI iEPA , code 0105990000 (ducks, geese, turkeys and guinea fowl over 185 g) with a CD of 20% will fall to 0 in T2, as will code 5109900000 concerning woollen threads. Vulcanised rubber clothing (code 4015900000), wallpapers (code 4814900000), folders for paper folders (code 4020300000) or silk fabrics (code 5007200000) will fall from 20% to 0 in T3.

2.2.4 – Conversely some products with low CDs (5% or 10%) will be excluded from liberalisation in the CI iEPA

While the vast majority of products excluded in the Ghana iEPA and WA EPA are taxed at least at 20%, many products that are taxed at 5% or 10% are excluded in the CI iEPA. For example, while the code 1006101000 concerning paddy seed will be liberalised in T3 in CI (in T5 in the WA EPA) the code 1006109000 concerning paddy other than seed taxed at 5% will be excluded. But since the Ghana iEPA has only 6-digit codes, the 100610 code taxed at 20% will remain excluded. This is even more common for codes at 10% of the CI iEPA.

2.2.5 – All of these differences in the timing of liberalisation and the level of CDs in CI and Ghana will inevitably lead to contraband exports

Most often the contraband will work from CI to Ghana, and sometimes the other way around when some TLs of Ghana are higher, and of course it will work too with the other ECOWAS States, given the laxity of its rules of origin, especially for agricultural products; and customs officers' 'understanding', which will be encouraged by contradictions in CDs levels. This understanding of WA customs officers is highlighted in many official and NGO reports, notably in the September 2017 WTO report on the trade policy review of WAEMU[43] and in the report of the

[43] https://www.wto.org/french/tratop_f/tpr_f/tp462_f.htm

USAID Hub for West Africa of September 2017[44]. The CI and Ghana iEPAs are thus a war machine against regional integration, which is a major objective of the regional EPA.

2.2.6 - The biggest question mark is how long CI and Ghana will apply the WA CET

Since the ECOWAS CET is different from the CET for EPA as there are no liberalised products in the absence of EPAs, CI should no longer apply the WA CET beyond 3 September 2018 nor should Ghana beyond 15 December 2021 for their imports from the EU, or it would mean that they will not comply with their iEPAs obligation to open their market to EU exports, which the EU exporters and DG Trade will surely not agree.

It is therefore necessary for both ECOWAS and the EU to take official action before 3 September 2018 – and they should even have done so before 3 February 2017 when a limited number of TLs should have already been liberalised – now that President Buhari of Nigeria has confirmed that his country will not sign the regional EPA. And, since Ghana should start opening its market to the EU only on 15 December 2021, smuggling will continue as well as regional disintegration. This will call into question the prospects for investment and competitiveness in the sectors, particularly the agricultural one, of all the ECOWAS States that planned to maintain in the long run a protection of 35% on their sensitive products in the hope that the regional EPA will be finalised.

Unless, miraculously, these chain destabilisation and the economic and political disintegration of WA lead the

---

[44] https://www.watradehub.com/wp-content/uploads/2017/08/COO-study-report-final.pdf

European Commission to abandon the implementation of the iEPAs and the WA EPA, if only by granting the status of GSP+ to CI, Ghana and Nigeria. Granting the GSP+ scheme to these countries depends only on the EU political will since they have signed or ratified the required 27 international conventions, except the one on the minimum age of access to employment for Ghana[45], which would not pose a problem for them to sign, even if its application is something totally different, as is the case of the Sahelian children working in cocoa plantations in CI.

However, the EU refused in 2008 to accede to Nigeria's request because it had not ratified the International Convention on Genocide, which it did in 2009 when a new request from Nigeria did not receive any response, for granting GSP+ to Nigeria is too bitter a pill to swallow, as it would ruin DG Trade's goal of implementing the regional EPA. That also explains DG Trade's pressure on CI and Ghana not to ask for this status but to ratify their IEPAs pending Nigeria's signing of the regional EPA which, as we know it since 9 April 2018, will not be the case.

---

[45] https://www.cepa.org.gh/resources/Ghana74.pdf

III – THE EU HAS REFUSED TO RELEASE THREE COMMISSIONED ASSESSMENTS ON THE IMPACTS OF THE WEST AFRICA EPA

DG Trade refused to release the last three impact assessments of the WA EPA that it had funded since their conclusions were negative for WA, but these were leaked[46]. Trade Commissioner Cecilia Malmström responded on 7 July 2016 to a request for clarification on this issue addressed by the French NGO CRIDEV on 16 May 2016, that "*The first two studies carried out by ITAQA in 2008 and 2012 were sponsored by the ECOWAS Commis*sion" and that "*these studies are now obsolete*", which is false since "sponsored" means "paid" in French law.

On the one hand, the European Commission logo appears at the top of the two ITAQA reports of April 2008 and April 2012, alongside the logos of ITAQA and ECOWAS, and the April 2008 report states that "*at the express request of the European Union, this mandate has been extended to cover also the analysis of the long-term consequences of the signing of possible Economic Partnership Agreements between the ECOWAS countries and the European Unio*n".

On the other hand, the Senegalese journalist Mohamed Gueye confirmed on 1 September 2008 in the newspaper

---

[46] http://www.bilaterals.org/?four-impact-studies-of-the-west&lang=en. In fact, the fourth study, from the University of Ibadan, was not financed by DG Trade but it also refused to mention it.

Le Quotidien that "*The Commission of the European Union, after commissioning a study on the consequences of the Economic Partnership Agreements (EPAs) in the African region of the Economic Community of West African States (ECOWAS), does not want to hear about the results of the latter, so much so that the consultants, who had been chosen in agreement with the ECOWAS Commission, are still running behind their money. Their misfortune? To have confirmed the thesis of those who have always maintained that EPAs are not good for the economies of developing countries*"[47].

An affirmation confirmed by e-mails from three CI researchers who contributed to the study (we do not give their names so as not to get them into trouble): one of them wrote to me: "*There has been a lot of debate between West Africa and EU parties about these reports. In the beginning, the European side talked about the study theoretically and technically to challenge the results. But, faced with the arguments put forward by West Africa and confirmed by those of Professor Decaluwé, they had to base the debate on a ground other than the purely scientific one*"; and the other researcher wrote to me: "*right from the beginning, there was an obvious bias in the objectives sought by this sponsored work, which we had pointed out!*".

As for the IFPRI study of January 2016, Commissioner Malmström wrote in her letter to CRIDEV: "*The report of the IFRI of January 2016 that you mention was not transmitted to my services*". This is another lie since

---

[47] Mohamed Gueye, *APE - Un modèle pour l'étude des Accords : Le Rapport que l'Europe refuse de reconnaître*, 9 September 2008. However the initial link is no longer working (http://www.plateforme-ane.sn/APE-Un-modele-pour-l-etude-des.html) but I can send you the article.

IFPRI wrote: "*This study was prepared at the request of the Chief Economist of DG Trade to provide an economic analysis in support of trade negotiations and trade policy issues related to the Economic Partnership Agreement between the EU and the West Africa-Economic Partnership Agreement Group*"[48].

48 http://www.ifpri.org/publication/european-unionwest-africa-economic-partnership-agreement

IV – THE UNTRUTHS ABOUT THE EU DEVELOPMENT AID TO THE WEST AFRICA EPA

4.1 - PAPED is only a relabelling of traditional EU aid funds

DG Trade has stated on numerous occasions that the EPA assistance program (PAPED) will grant € 6.5 bn to WA from 2015 to 2020 while DG Development and Cooperation (DEVCO) pointed out in June 2015 that this is a simple retargeting of the aid already programmed by the EDF (European Development Fund), the EIB (European Investment Bank) and normal funds from the European Development Cooperation, so that there are no additional specific funds for the EPA[49].

Jacques Gallezot's report of 25 November 2016 on the Competitiveness Observatory in the context of the EU-WA EPA has recognised this triple source of funding[50] and DG Trade has eventually acknowledged it on 29 November 2017: "*The Council of Ministers decided on 17 March 2014 to allocate at least € 6.5 billion to the PAPED, using all available financial instruments, including those of the EU Member States and the EIB*"[51].

Among the recent pressures on Nigeria to sign, the EU Ambassador to Nigeria and ECOWAS, Michel Arrion,

49 https://ec.europa.eu/europeaid/sites/devco/files/epa-brochure_en.pdf
50 http://trade.ec.europa.eu/doclib/docs/2017/february/tradoc_155303.pdf
51 http://trade.ec.europa.eu/doclib/docs/2014/july/tradoc_152694.pdf

said the EU pledges to fund the PAPED to the tune of € 6,5 bn every 5 years until 2035[52]. An unfounded promise since the Cotonou Agreement expires in 2020 and it is not known whether it will be renewed and with what budget, and in any case not until 2035 since the EU Budget is not programmed beyond 2020. Not to mention that the United Kingdom (UK), which will leave the EU, contributes 14.5% to the 11th EDF which is not an EU budget but is financed by Member States.

In the aforementioned document of 29 November 2017, DG Trade made the same non-binding promise that "*The EU has agreed to continue to assist West Africa throughout the implementation process, so that EU support will also continue beyond 2019 ... EU support will focus on trade, agriculture, infrastructure, energy and capacity building for civil society. existing needs, as the West African Authorities have estimated*". An unwarranted assertion!

Similarly for the EU-EAC EPA, according to SEATINI, "*Article 75.4 of the EAC-EU EPA stipulates that any development cooperation or support to the EPA development matrix will be ensured and implemented by existing EU mechanisms, in particular the European Development Fund (EDF) and in the framework of the successive relevant instruments financed from the EU general budget. So, it is clear that there is no commitment for additional resources in the EU-EAC EPA*"[53].

---

[52] http://leadership.ng/news/496017/eu-appeals-fg-ratify-economic-partnership-agreement; http://www.bilaterals.org/?eu-threatens-to-stop-market-access

[53] SEATINI, *The EAC-EU EPA: Tanzania is raising pertinent issues*, 4 March 2017, http://www.bilaterals.org/?the-eac-eu-epa-tanzania-is-raising

4.2 - Lack of credibility of EU aid to offset the net fiscal impact of the EPA

An equally unwarranted promise comes from article 60 of the WA EPA that "*West Africa undertakes to establish tax reforms as part of the change in taxation resulting from liberalisation. The European Union undertakes to help West Africa to implement these reforms. In view of these reforms, the European Union undertakes to provide funding to cover the fiscal impact agreed by the Parties for the period of tariff dismantling*"[54].

But how could WA put in place tax reforms offsetting the huge losses in customs revenues (CRs: CDs+VAT) on imports and the loss of competitiveness of its companies linked to the market opening to 76.2% of EU28-UK (to account for Brexit) exports, a figure identified by SOL on the basis of 2015 EU-UK exports, but which will increase significantly with the diversion of trade to the EU as imports from third countries would continue to be taxed. The losses in CRs will be even larger as the EPA prohibits to raise export taxes without the EU consent (Article 13), and while they exceed the import CRs in CI and Guinea Bissau, and that the WA population would increase by 65% from 2017 to 2037 and by 118% to 2050.

Jacques Gallezot's report on the Observatory of competitiveness in the WA EPA is more directive: "*It will be necessary to improve the management of public revenue and expenditure in order to compensate for temporary losses of tax revenue. This will include, among other things, ensuring the necessary fiscal transition, including enhancing the domestic tax take (with a substantial reduction in exemptions), optimising the*

[54] http://data.consilium.europa.eu/doc/document/ST-13370-2014-INIT/fr/pdf

collection system, and fighting against customs and port fraud. It will also be necessary to strengthen the monitoring of public revenue and expenditure. The urgent need to rationalise the management of public funds in connection with the implementation of the EPA should encourage the states in the region to identify and implement relevant and necessary reforms for a progressive and sustainable integration in the global economy". It is clearly known that this "*progressive and sustainable integration in the global economy*" implies the reduction of CDs!

While recognising in Article 102 of the EU-EAC EPA text that EU financial assistance will come from three sources – the 11th EDF, the EIB and the EU's Cooperation Budget – Article 100 makes the same promises to cover revenue losses related to the EPA: "*With regard to revenue losses linked to the reduction of tariffs, the EU shall... c) provide financial resources to cover transitionally the agreed losses of government revenue arising from elimination and or substantial reduction in customs tariffs*". These promises are less likely to have a greater impact on the decline in EAC customs revenue than in WA. Indeed, while the UK's share of WA exports to EU28 was only 9.4% in 2015, it accounted for 17.9% of EAC exports to the EU28-UK, 38.5% of which being from Kenya.

However, at the request of DG Trade, ITAQA simulated in its April 2012 report the impact of the PAPED on the results of the EPA on the following bases: "*1) All PAPED expenditures are generated by new foreign resource flows. 2) PAPED resources are independent and additional to tax neutralisation transfers. 3) Two identical and successive PAPEDs are implemented: from 2011 to 2015 and from 2016 to 2020, repeating the same program, and now the value of the expenses*".

The conclusions of ITAQA were that, by comparing the evolution with EPA and without EPA of the base scenario where the 3 non-LDC DCs are subject to the GSP or MFN regime and the LDCs to the EBA regime, the annual transfers necessary to compensate the loss of customs revenue due to the liberalisation would increase from $ 182 M at the start of liberalisation (2017) to $ 1.491 bn at the end (2040). And, despite the two successive PAPED – 2011-15 and 2016-20 – at the end of the liberalisation there would still be a need for transfers of $ 761 M so that the public revenues would not fall with the EPA compared to the basic scenario. And these needs would appear at the end of the second PAPED, with $ 250 M in 2021. We can better understand why Commissioner Cecilia Malmström wrote to CRIDEV that "*these ITAQA studies are now obsolete*"!

As for the IFPRI study of January 2016, also sponsored by DG Trade, it is also based on the assumption that the PAPED would be renewed from 2015 to 2035, or by € 1.3 bn per year, but its impact would not be significant since it would be allocated both in the EPA scenario and in the baseline scenario without EPAs (with the GSP scheme for the three DCs, the GSP+ scheme for Cape Verde and the EBA scheme for the 12 LDCs). That is an implicit way of recognising that the PAPED is only the new label for the traditional funds of EU development aid with the free assumption that it would be renewed until the end of liberalisation.

Yet, despite the extension of the PAPED until 2035, IFPRI anticipates that a tax would still be needed to maintain the fiscal revenues, which would otherwise be reduced by liberalisation due to the EPA. The conclusion of the study is that "*The EPA agreement raises the issue of a fiscal adjustment. Custom tariffs represent an important part of public revenues in ECOWAS countries. However, the EPA entails a significant reduction of custom duties, since the EU is an important and significant trading partner in the region. To maintain public expenses and the provision of public goods constant, ECOWAS governments will have to find an alternative source of public revenues... which necessarily reduces welfare... In conclusion, the benefits of the EPA between the EU and the EU countries seem weak, even negative*"[55].

It is therefore understandable why Commissioner Cecilia Malmström replied to CRIDEV that "*The IFRI report of January 2016 that you mention has not been sent to my services*"!

4.3 – **Bilateral and multilateral safeguards will benefit the EU much more**

Bilateral safeguards would only occur in the EPA in the event of large increases in the quantities imported, but not in the event of a fall in import prices. However, in the current context of high volatility of prices and euro exchange rate – which is also that of the CFA franc for the eight WA States grouped in the WAEMU (Economic and Monetary Union of West Africa) and the six states of CEMAC (Economic and Monetary Community of Central Africa) – a price-related safeguard is essential.

On the other hand, the WA EPA provides for the EU to take exceptional safeguard measures when "*the average Community white sugar price is for two consecutive months lower than 80% of the average Community white sugar price recorded during the previous marketing year*", although this provision does not appear in the main text of the WA EPA but is disguised in paragraph 3 of Annex B

[55] http://www.ifpri.org/publication/european-unionwest-africa-economic-partnership-agreement

of the EPA. And, while the safeguards invoked by WA must prove a serious injury to the companies concerned, the EU is not obliged to prove that the EU sugar producers have suffered injury or that WA was at the origin of the fall in the sugar price. In fact this would be difficult presently because WA is facing a sugar deficit, particularly from the EU which exported to WA 75,070 heavily subsidised tonnes in 2016.

When the conditions impose these quantitative safeguards, ECOWAS member States must submit to the Joint EU-WA EPA Committee proofs of the damage caused to the concerned sector. The temporary remedies provided may consist of a suspension of the reduction of CDs programmed on this product, an increase in CDs not exceeding those applied to other countries, or tariff quotas not exceeding two years. Even if all ECOWAS States are WTO members and therefore have bound duties [56], ECOWAS itself is not a WTO Member and the CET has only applied duties which will therefore be the maximum CDs that ECOWAS members could apply, at least as long as they stay in ECOWAS and apply its CET.

As for multilateral safeguards, article 21 of the WA EPA and the infant industry clause of Article 23 provide that the EU will not use for more than five years the GATT safeguards of Article XIX, the safeguards of the Agreement on Safeguards and the Special Safeguard Clause of Article 5 of the Agreement on Agriculture (AoA) – a clause that is not available to WA because only the WTO Members having bound all their tariff lines in the GATT before the creation of WTO have had access to them –, which implies that the EU may use them later.

---

[56] Bound duties are the maximum level that can be reached by the applied duties, which gives WTO member States considerable flexibility to vary their level depending on market conditions.

Peter Lunenborg of the South Centre[57] emphasises that multilateral safeguards and the infant industry clause cannot be used by WA member States individually but only by the "*West Africa Party*" which Article 99 of the EU-WA EPA defines as follows: "*The West Africa Party comprises ECOWAS, UEMOA, and their Member States within their respective areas of competence as derived from the ECOWAS and UEMOA Treaties, and Mauritania*". It would be very difficult to find an agreement between all these components, especially since they will have to apply the safeguards in the same way and "*on the basis of the non-preferential rules of origin of the parties*" that WA has not defined, implying that they would be those of the EU or the WTO, in other words these safeguards would be inapplicable. Admittedly, for CI and Ghana iEPAs, multilateral safeguards will be simpler to decide, but they will also have to be applied "*on the basis of non-preferential rules of origin of the parties*", which they have not defined either.

No reference is made in the WA EPA to the ECOWAS Supplementary Protection Tax (SPT), a surcharge on the CET applicable to products imported from third countries in case of increased volumes of imports of at least 25% of the average of the last three years for which data are available, as well as in case of price increases if, in a given month, the average CIF price of a product falls below 80% the average CIF price of the last three years for which data are available. Each ECOWAS State can set the level of SPT up to 70% of its bound MFN CDs in the WTO. The WA EPA or the iEPAs would thus prevent the use of SPT for imports from the EU, in contradiction with regional integration.

---

[57] Peter Lunenborg, *Analysis of the West Africa EPA*, South Centre, Geneva, February 2017.

4.4 – **The EU cannot pledge not to subsidise its agricultural exports to West Africa**

Paragraph 6 of Article 48 of the WA EPA provides: "*The European Union Party undertakes to refrain from the use of export subsidies for agricultural products exported to West Africa*", which does not correspond to a definitive commitment not to use them. Indeed, despite that the EU pledged to no longer use export refunds at the WTO Ministerial conference of Nairobi in December 2015 and confirmed it on 6 October 2017[58], nevertheless it does not seem that this commitment has changed the EU regulation No 1308/2013 of 17 December 2013 providing that "*Refunds on exports to third countries, based on the difference between prices within the Union and on the world market, and falling within the limits set by the commitments made within the WTO, should be retained as a measure which may cover certain products to which this Regulation applies where the conditions in the internal market are such as those described for exceptional measures*"[59].

But the real issue relates to domestic subsidies. It is an EU recurring position, defended at the WTO, that its domestic subsidies to exported products are not making any dumping, are not export subsidies, and even more so as the vast majority of them are decoupled from the level of production or price and are notified in the WTO green box[60].

---

[58] http://trade.ec.europa.eu/doclib/press/index.cfm?id=1738

[59] http://eur-lex.europa.eu/legal-content/EN/TXT/PDF/?uri=CELEX:32013R1308&from=en

[60] *The EU actual agricultural supports (AMS and OTDS) in 2013-14*, SOL, 29 April 2017, https://www.sol-asso.fr/wp-content/uploads/

This also applies to animal products that benefit from highly subsidised feeds to the EU-produced cereals, oilseed meals and pulses (COPs). If they are COPs producers who receive the decoupled direct aids to feed – 'single payment scheme' (SPS) until 2016 and 'basic payment scheme' (BPS) since –, the producers of animal products – particularly pork, poultry and eggs who do not get direct payments as those producing beef, mutton and dairy – receive implicit but actual subsidies corresponding to the lower prices they pay for COPs of EU origin. Indeed these prices would be much higher in the absence of the BPS received by the producers of COPs to compensate for the reduction of their administered prices which occurred in the CAP reforms of 1992 and 1999.

Yet the WTO Appellate Body has ruled four times – in the case of the Dairy Products of Canada of December 2001 and December 2002; in the US Cotton case of March 2005 and the EU Sugar Case of April 2005 – that domestic subsidies to exported agricultural products are to be taken into account in assessing dumping. In particular in the EU Sugar case, the Appellate Body stated: "*279. WTO Members are entitled to provide 'domestic support' to agricultural producers within the limits of their domestic subsidy commitments.*[61] *We observe, however, that the Appellate Body has also held that economic effects of WTO-consistent domestic support may 'spill over' to benefit export production. Such spill-over effects may arise, in particular, in circumstances where agricultural products result from a single line of production that does not distinguish between production destined for the*

2017/01/The-EU-actual-agriculrural-supports-AMS-and-OTDS-in-2013-14.pdf

[61] Appellate Body Report, *Canada – Dairy (Article 21.5 – New Zealand and US)*, para. 88. (original emphasis)

domestic market and production destined for the export market. 280. In this respect, the Appellate Body has cautioned that, "if domestic support could be used, without limit, to provide support for exports, it would undermine the benefits intended to accrue through a WTO Member's export subsidy commitments."[62] *We believe that these statements are relevant to the present case. In this case, we note that C sugar is produced and exported in huge quantities, and that there is a considerable difference between the world market price and the average total cost of production of sugar in the European Communities*".

SOL has carried out numerous evaluations of the EU dumping of agricultural exports to ACP countries, of which those to WA. The EU28 exported 3.4 million tonnes (Mt) of cereals in 2016 (including those incorporated in processed cereal products) through domestic subsidies of € 203.7 M, with a dumping rate of 36.6% on the raw cereals exported[63]. It also exported 2.5 Mt of dairy products in milk equivalent thanks to € 168.6 M in subsidies and at an average dumping rate of 20.8%[64]. In 2016, the EU28 subsidies to its agricultural exports to CI amounted to € 99.9 M, of which € 42 M to cereals (dumping rate of 30.2%), €34.9 M to beef, € 11.7 M to

---

[62] Appellate Body Report, *Canada – Dairy (Article 21.5 – New Zealand and US)*, para. 91.

[63] *The subsidies to the EU exports of cereal products to West Africa in 2015 and 2016*, SOL, March 17, 2017; https://www.sol-asso.fr/wp-content/uploads/2017/01/The-subsidies-to-the-EU-exports-of-cereal-products-to-West-Africa-in-2015-and-2016-February-172017.pdf

[64] *The huge dumping of extra-EU exports of dairy products and to the EPAs of West Africa, SADC, CEMAC and EAC in 2016*, SOL, April 11, 2017, https://www.sol-asso.fr/wp-content/uploads/2017/01/The-huge-dumping-of-extra-EU-exports-of-dairy-products-and-to-the-4-African-EPAS.pdf

dairy products (dumping rate of 16.4%) and € 11.3 M to pork[38].

4.5 – **From customs duties to total agricultural protection**

Paragraph 3 of Annex A of the Doha Work Program (known as the Framework Agreement) of the WTO General Council of 31 July 2004 on the 'Framework for the Establishment of Modalities for Agriculture' states: "*The reforms in all three pillars form an interconnected whole and must be approached in a balanced and equitable manner*". These three pillars are market access (i.e. import protection), export competition (i.e. export subsidies) and domestic support.

This implies that import protection must include domestic subsidies as they have an import substitution effect and a dumping effect by allowing products to be exported below the average national total cost of production without subsidy. Which implies in turn that one must add to the tariff – converted into ad valorem equivalent (AVE) in the case of specific tariff (per tonne or head of livestock) or mixed (ad valorem + specific), which dominate for agricultural products imported by the EU – the AVE of subsidies to obtain the total protection rate. The WTO report on 'World Trade in 2012'[65] cites the work of Kee et al. 2008, according to whom "*For products subject to agricultural domestic support, in 36% of these tariff lines the AVE of agricultural domestic support is higher than the tariff... The countries with the highest*

65 https://www.wto.org/english/res_e/booksp_e/anrep_e/world_trade_report12_e.pdf

AVEs of domestic support are European Union members"[66].

SOL has shown that, for low and medium quality soft wheat, milk powder, liquid condensed milk, frozen offal of chicken, beef and pork imported by EU28 in 2016, the total protection rate including domestic subsidies was in AVE of respectively 73.6%, 102.4%, 127.4%, 74.2%, 288.4% and 40%[67]. Rates to be compared to the CDs of the WA CET for these same products that the EU28 exported extensively in WA in 2016 and 2017, of respectively 5%, 5%, 10% or 20%, 35%, 35% %, 35%, these last 3 rates falling to 20% for the iEPAs of CI and Ghana. In addition, the CDs of wheat and milk powder will drop to 0 as soon as liberalisation begins.

In addition to taking into account subsidies to assess the total agricultural protection rate, the WTO rules only take into account sector-specific subsidies, here agricultural subsidies, and the only year in progress, or at best the last few years. That is why SOL (formerly Solidarité) proposed at the WTO Ministerial Conference in Hong Kong in December 2005 to put in a 'gold box' all types of past and present non-agricultural support and past agricultural support [68]. Indeed, the higher current competitiveness of Western agri-food products, especially of the EU, compared to those of developing countries (DCs), especially of ACP countries, is much less the result

---

66 https://www.wto.org/french/res_f/booksp_f/anrep_f/world_trade_report12_f.pdf

67 *From customs duties to total agricultural protection: the case of the European Union-West Africa trade*, SOL, April 19, 2018, https://www.sol-asso.fr/analyses-politiques-agricoles-jacques-b-2018/

68 *The green box: a black box which hides the gold box*, Solidarité, December 6, 2005, https://www.wto.org/english/forums_e/ngo_e/posp56_e.htm

of the gap in their current level of tariffs and/or agricultural subsidies – all the more so when calculated per capita or full-time AWU (agricultural worker unit) equivalent – than of current and past non-agricultural support and past agricultural support, for decades and even centuries, including strong import protection and domestic and export subsidies, as well as export taxes.

That is why, even if the WTO decided stricter criteria for the green box, developed countries could still increase their gold box subsidies to maintain the competitiveness of their farmers and agri-food industries. They will always find the means to ensure their food sovereignty. In particular, instead of maintaining specific agricultural institutions, it will be sufficient to integrate them into larger institutions so that the specific nature of subsidies will disappear and could not be sued at the WTO.

These huge differences in the total protection rate and the unilateral ability of the EU to maintain its food sovereignty under all circumstances on its staple food products should open its eyes to the fact that imposing EPAs to WA can only backfire on itself by pushing WA further into misery and encouraging its millions of young people without future to migrate to the EU and swell the ranks of the jihadist movements.

V – The EU seems to ignore WA huge development challenges

While the effects of the EPAs have not yet been felt in WA, the region is already facing enormous challenges in all sectors of activity. In addition to the macroeconomic challenges, WA will be confronted mainly with the three major challenges of population explosion, climate change and food deficit, whilst about 60% of its population depend on agriculture. To that will be added the fact that, contrary to the claims by the European Commission, the EU itself is facing a huge structural food deficit.

5.1 – Macroeconomic challenges

The African Development Bank (AfDB) highlights in its WA outlook for 2018 that *"To reduce vulnerability to external shocks caused by the dependence of several economies, especially that of Nigeria, on oil or other mineral extraction, West Africa must increase domestic input into its products through manufacturing, especially processing minerals and agricultural products. Inflation has run in double digits since 2015, hindering growth. External debt has increased as economic growth fell with the decline in world commodity prices in 2015-16... Poverty is high, with 43 percent of the population below the international $1.90 per day poverty line in 2013 (the most recent estimate)... The business environment shapes the formal sector, which creates few decent jobs. In the normal course of structural transformation, labor shifts from agriculture to manufacturing to services. That* *transition has stalled in West Africa due to customs problems, unavailability of finance, high taxes and heavy burdens of tax accounting, rigid regulation by a low-quality bureaucracy, and inadequate energy and transport infrastructure. The consequence is an atrophying formal sector and a booming informal sector*[69]".

And despite the fact that the eight member States of the WAEMU (West African Economic and Monetary Union) out of the 16 ECOWAS States, have seen much better results in terms of both GDP, inflation and budget deficit, the WTO report on WAEMU Trade Policy Review underlines nevertheless that "*In 2016 almost 5 out of 10 of them live below the poverty line*"[70].

5.2 – **The demographic challenge**

The demographic challenge is immense since, according to projections by the United Nations Population Organisation in its 2017 revision, the population of WA would be multiplied by 2.18 from 2017 to 2050 (from 372 to 810 million, M). Since the EU28 population would fall very slightly (from 509 to 503 M), that of WA would exceed it by 2030. A fortiori the Brexit will reduce to 427.4 M the EU27 population in 2050[71]. This will

---

69 https://www.google.fr/search?q=West+Africa+economic+outlook+2018&rlz=1C1CHBD_frFR795FR795&oq=West+Africa+economic+outlook+2018&aqs=chrome..69i57j69i60.22462j0j7&sourceid=chrome&ie=UTF-8

70 https://www.wto.org/french/tratop_f/tpr_f/g362_f.pdf

71 However, Brexit will not be included in this book, assuming that the UK will establish bilateral relations with ACP countries similar to those of the rest of EU.

inevitably change the geopolitical balance of power between WA and the EU.

Although there will be an explosion in the urban population, Bruno Dorin of CIRAD anticipates an increase of 167 million agricultural workers in sub-Saharan Africa from 2006 to 2050, the only sub-continent where it would increase[72]. And the US Population Reference Bureau emphasises that "*With a fertility rate higher than the average of the continent, it is West Africa that will carry along the African population growth.*[73]" Countries like Mali, Burkina Faso Faso or Niger will see their population multiplied by more than 2.5 by 2050. It is also in Niger that fertility is the highest in the world: 7.6 children per woman on average.

5.3 – <u>The climate challenge</u>

According to the United Nations Environment Program (UNEP), a two-degree warming would reduce the total agricultural output of Sub-Saharan Africa (SSA) by 10% in 2050, and a higher warming, more likely, would reduce it by 15 to 20%[74]. UNEP states that an increase of 1.2 to 1.9 degrees would be sufficient to increase the number of undernourished Africans, already estimated at 240 M by 25% in Central Africa, 50% in East Africa, and 95% in

---

72 http://www.alimenterre.org/sites/www.cfsi.asso.fr/files/877-dynamiques_agricoles_en_afrique_subsaharienne_1961-2050.pdf

73 http://www.rfi.fr/afrique/20150820-afrique-connaitre-forte-croissance-demographique-2050-nigeria-monde

74 Richard Munang and Jesica Andrews, "*L'Afrique face au changement climatique*", PNUE, 2014 http://www.un.org/africarenewal/fr/magazine/%C3%A9dition-sp%C3%A9ciale-agriculture-2014/l%E2%80%99afrique-face-au-changement-climatique

WA[75]. According to climate change impact analyses, reported by AfricaInteract, "*a 2% increase in temperature is likely to lead to the disappearance of 10 to 15% of species in West Africa, and would affect agricultural production in Africa by 30%*"[76].

However UNEP also emphasises that a rapid conversion of SSA agriculture to agro-ecological practices would limit these threats and increase yields: "*In July 2013, African leaders made the ambitious commitment to eradicate hunger by 2025. They intend to encourage farmers to gradually abandon yield farming, fragile farming systems and crops requiring large amounts of fertilisers and pesticides, in favour of sustainable practices that are resilient to climate change*"[77].

FAO shares the same views: "*High-input, resource-intensive farming systems, which have caused massive deforestation, water scarcities, soil depletion and high levels of greenhouse gas emissions, cannot deliver sustainable food and agricultural production. Needed are innovative systems that protect and enhance the natural resource base, while increasing productivity... such as agroecology, ago-forestry, climate-smart agriculture and conservation agriculture, which also build upon indigenous and traditional knowledge*"[78].

Numerous other analyses, among which those of Olivier De Schutter[79], have called into question the so-

---

[75] Ibid.

[76] http://www.hubrural.org/Agriculture-et-changement.html?lang=fr

[77] Ibid.

[78] FAO, "*The future of food and agriculture – Trends and challenges*", 2017, page X, http://www.fao.org/3/a-i6583e.pdf

[79] Olivier De Schutter, "*The political economy of food systems reform*", European Review of Agricultural Economics Volume 44, Issue 4, 1 September 2017, Pages 705–731, https://doi.org/10.1093/erae/jbx009

called 'modern' agribusiness-type production systems that are highly intensive in capital and chemical inputs, with their negative impact on the environment and agricultural employment in SSA, all the more so when accompanied by land grabbing from traditional peasants. However, most official African institutions like the African Development Bank (AfDB) are hindering this conversion and advocating for a conventional intensification based on subsidies to chemical fertilisers[80].

5.4 – <u>The food deficit challenge</u>

If the WA food trade deficit vis-à-vis all countries – in SITC codes that include fish but exclude non-food agricultural products – was maximum in 2011, at € 8.6 bn, it fell sharply until 2016 (€ 718 M) thanks to the falling prices of imported food products. On the other hand, excluding trade in coffee-cocoa-spices – which are not staple foods and are mainly exported – the food deficit of WA was multiplied by 10.9 in 2016 (at € 7.851 bn).

Senegal's total production of dry cereals – millet, sorghum, maize, fonio – increased by only 4.2% from 2000-2004 to 2011-15 – of which 11.6% for millet, but stagnated for maize and decreased by 16.5% for sorghum –, while the population increased by 53.4% from 2000 (9.861 M) to 2015 (15.129 M). Although rice production (paddy) has increased 2.7 times between these two periods, the production of all cereals (paddy included) rose by only 36.4%.

---

[80] ADB, "*Feeding Africa: Strategy for Agricultural Transformation in Africa 2016-2025*", May 2016, https://www.afdb.org/fileadmin/uploads/afdb/Documents/Generic-Documents/Feed_Africa-_Strategy_for_Agricultural_Transformation_in_Africa_2016-2025.pdf

As for the Senegalese per capita consumption of wheat – a cereal that WA can only very marginally produce and at a very high cost –, it has risen from 22 kg in 2000 to 32 kg in 2015, whereas the consumption of dry cereals has dropped from 88 kg to 61 kg, of which 36.9 kg of millet, 15.6 kg of maize, 8.4 kg of sorghum and 152 g of fonio. On the other hand, rice consumption (production + imports) per capita increased from 68 to 93 kg.

The increase in wheat consumption – in the form of bread, pasta, couscous and cakes – is not sustainable in the long run because the price of wheat will rise sharply due to stagnant yields in producing countries and the rise in consumption in the countries of West Asia, the Middle East and the Maghreb which, unlike WA, cannot grow alternatives products such as tropical cereals and tubers. It is therefore suicidal for the long run to have reduced from 5% to 0 the CDs on cereal imports, mainly wheat, from the EU in the WA EPA and the iEPAs of CI and Ghana.

Especially since there is a strong potential for increasing local cereals yields, but we must avoid promoting production systems based intensively on chemical inputs. If we compare the evolution in WA and in Ethiopia, we can see that the yield of millet in WA decreased from 781 kg/ha from 2000-03 to 728 kg in 2009-13 while that of sorghum increased from 888 kg to 978 kg and that of maize from 1415 kg to 1691 kg. In Ethiopia, on the other hand, the increases ranged from 962 kg to 1699 kg for millet, from 1267 kg to 2169 kg for sorghum and from 1746 to 3079 kg for maize.

WA should therefore reduce wheat consumption in favour of new recipes from maize (such as tortillas which are widely consumed in Mexico and Central America), but also from cassava (as can be seen in many culinary examples in Brazil, including pizza made from cassava) and from millet and sorghum as well.

5.5 – The EU itself is facing a huge structural food deficit

We must demystify the assertion by the European Commission that the EU has a duty to help feed the world, an assertion based on the assimilation of its agricultural trade to its food trade. While its agricultural surplus reached a peak of € 20.5 bn in 2017, its food deficit was € 5.5 bn[81]. This can be explained by the fact that the European Commission does not count the huge growing deficit in fish and preparations, which reached € 20.2 billion in 2017 because they are not agricultural products according to the WTO.

Moreover, since the EU has a structural food surplus on developed countries, € 15.9 bn in 2017, its structural food deficit vis-à-vis developing countries was € 21.4 bn. And, if we do not count the huge EU surplus in drinks - which are not staple foods -, its food deficit vis-à-vis developing countries was € 31.9 bn.

The EU has clearly a significant and growing food deficit vis-à-vis WA – from € 2 M in 2010 to € 2.7 bn in 2017, and, excluding drinks, from € 2.2 bn to € 3.2 bn – but, if imports of cocoa, coffee and spices, which are not basic food products in WA, are excluded, the EU food surplus over WA shows an increase from € 1.4 bn in 2010 to € 1.8 bn in 2017.

---

81 https://www.sol-asso.fr/wp-content/uploads/2017/01/The-truth-about-the-European-Union-food-defcit-and-the-dumping-impact-of-its-domestic-subsdies-June-26-2018.pdf

VI – The pseudo-scientific evaluation of DG Trade on the impact of WA EPA

Having rejected the negative conclusions of the three impact studies conducted by the consultancy firms it had selected and financed, DG Trade carried out its own study published in March 2016, while using the same expert from IFPRI, David Laborde, who had already participated in the three rejected previous studies. As a matter of fact, DG Trade considers essential the use of a computable general equilibrium model to validate politically determined results so as to provide political authorities with what would look like an irrefutable scientific truth. And this is the practice in all its bilateral free trade agreements.

6.1 – <u>The demystification of general equilibrium models by Jean-Marc Boussard</u>

Specialist of models applied in the analysis of agricultural policies and former Chairperson of the French Rural Economy Society and of the Union of European Academies of Agriculture, Jean-Marc Boussard has long demystified presuppositions and conclusions. He observed in 2000 that "*everywhere in the world, computable general equilibrium models (CGEMs) serve as a hammer to drive the nail of liberalism*"[82]. One of these CGEMs, GTAP, "*will exert a great influence on all the people who will use it in believing that the reality is in line with this model, especially on many negotiators in the upcoming WTO negotiations. When working on this model... they will learn very quickly that everything that comes close to liberalisation is 'good', everything that moves away from it is 'bad'*". However "*the 'standard MCEGs'... presented as oracles responsible for saying good economic policies... (have) two major flaws: first, to unduly favour liberalisation... then, to neglect the essential aspects of economic dynamics*".

Because the basic assumptions of these models – measurability and comparability of usefulness between individuals without interference with each other, prices as sole information signals – "*are not verified because it is quite impossible to aggregate preferences*" and it is not particularly credible to believe that the countries which will be winners in the liberalisation process will compensate the losing ones, as would be the case for Africa in a number of scenarios or, more broadly, that the winners within one country will compensate the losers. Thus, the World Bank study on the impact of the WA EPA on Nigeria, which was quoted by DG Trade, concluded that "*the impact is slightly regressive because it is the wealthier households that benefit more from it since EU-imported products that benefit from the EPA are part of their usual shopping list*"[83].

---

[82] Jean-Marc Boussard, *Agriculture, équilibre général et OMC. Une vision critique des modèles utilisés dans les négociations*, Economie Rurale, n°257, mai-juin 2000, p.3-16.

[83] http://documents.worldbank.org/curated/en/411251468324859303/ECOWAS-economic-partnership-agreement-with-the-EU-and-Nigerian-trade-and-development

According to Jean-Marc Boussard, another major flaw in CGEMs is their static nature and the ability of entrepreneurs to make 'rational projections', particularly in terms of price. However, "*thinking that they can accurately predict equilibrium prices in twenty years is a dream. In fact, no empirical study has ever shown that traders in a market were able to predict what the equilibrium price would be next year!*". But "*if markets are operating poorly based on false expectations, chances are that the space of possibilities and trade will shrink instead of expanding. In addition, risk considerations reinforce this idea*". Boussard concluded by wondering "*if the excessive liberalism of the Uruguay Round negotiators will not lead to a surge of global violence,*" which seemed to have been a premonitory observation.

6.2 – The main weaknesses of the GTAP-9 model

The impact assessment of the WA EPA by DG Trade[84], which mainly focused on the reduction of customs duties (CDs), is based on the most recent CGEM: "*The database used was the Global Trade Analysis Project-GTAP 9, a fully documented, publicly available global database which contains complete bilateral trade information, transport and protection linkages among 140 regions for all 57 GTAP commodities for 2011*".

But this GTAP-9 is far from complete and reliable for WA, for the following reasons:

- It covers only 7 of the 15 ECOWAS countries – the 8 others are grouped in "the rest of ECOWAS" – even if they represent the bulk of the population and GDP of WA,

84 http://trade.ec.europa.eu/doclib/docs/2016/april/tradoc_154422.pdf

and the impact on poverty and inequality is only based on two countries (Nigeria and Ghana).
- Although DG Trade asserts that its model is based on the most recent data for WA, including the CET (Common External Tariff) of ECOWAS in force since January 2015, the GTAP-9 data for WA are based on country Input-Output Tables (IOTs) derived from much older and disparate social accounting matrices per country: 1998 for CI, 2003 for Benin, 2005 for Burkina Faso, Guinea and Senegal, 2006 for Nigeria and Togo[85]. And the data of these IOTs are very different from one country to another: the number of products included ranges from 29 in Benin and Nigeria to 30 in Guinea, Senegal and Togo, 34 in CI and 41 in Ghana. The number of raw and processed agricultural products varies even more: 6 in CI and Nigeria, 7 in Benin and Togo, 11 in Guinea, 12 in Burkina and Ghana. Price sources are unknown in Nigeria and Benin.
- While both ECOWAS and EU TLs are at 8 or 10 digits, DG Trade admits that "*the rules of origin themselves are normally defined at the 4-digit LT level of the Harmonised System, which is a finer level of aggregation than the level of the GTAP sectors to which the simulations are conducted*", which implies that they are conducted at the 2-digit aggregated level!
- Since January 2015, the current ECOWAS CET is based on the 2012 Harmonised System (HS) nomenclature for the designation and codification of goods[86]. The 5,899

---

85 https://www.gtap.agecon.purdue.edu/resources/download/7642.pdf

86 WTO, *Trade policy review of the WAEMU*, Report by the Secretariat, https://docs.wto.org/dol2fe/Pages/FE_Search/FE_S_S009-DP.aspx?Language=E&CatalogueIdList=243443,238700,110265,101133,72924,42906&CurrentCatalogueIdIndex=0&FullTextHash=371857150

TLs are distributed as follows: 85 TLs at the rate of 0% for essential social goods; 2,146 TLs at a rate of 5% on basic raw materials and capital goods; 1,373 TLs at the rate of 10% for intermediate products; 2,165 TLs at a rate of 20% for final consumer goods; and 130 TLs at the rate of 35% on "specific goods for economic development".

But the CET has evolved: that of 2011 was composed of 5,550 TLs at 10 digits, according to the HS 2007 nomenclature. The worst is that the tariff offer on which the WA EPA text is based only contained 5,127 TLs because, according to a South Centre's analysis, "t*his is what emerges from the 'Memo on the offer to access the West African Goods Market' prepared by the ECOWAS Commission for the meeting for the Experts of the Ministerial Committee on EPA negotiations, which took place from 20-22 February 2013 in Accra. Paragraph 28 of this document indicates that the value of trade of the proposed West African offer is based on calculations of the arithmetic mean during the reference period of 2002-2004, and that these statistics were jointly adopted by the two parties for the EPA negotiations. In other words the tariff offers and the current West Africa EPA market access schedule are based on negotiated trade data, rather than actual trade data which date back to more than 10 years ago. The same paragraph also states that the West African offer is based on the 2012 version of the Harmonised System (HS 2012). It is not known how the negotiated trade data covering 2002 to 2004, expressed either in HS1996 or HS2002 (two or three versions earlier than the HS2012), were converted into HS2012. This is an important technical detail, as the many changes that occurred between HS1996/2002 and HS2012 might affect* *the statistic on the percentage of liberalisation in terms of value*"[87].

- All this makes it very difficult to know on which years and what level of CDs the results of the DG Trade study are based. Moreover, it does not give actual figures but only percentages of the variation between the impact with EPA and that without EPA.

- There is only one household per country to represent consumers, driven solely by the desire to maximise their 'welfare' through the lowest retail prices. Only one household per country represents all the producers, with the sole aim of maximising their profits in the short run as if these behaviours were common in WA where the informal sector brings together more than 90% of the population, and where the first concern of the 60% of the population working in micro-family farms is to be self-sufficient in terms of food before thinking about selling, let alone exporting.

- Like in all general or partial equilibrium models, that of DG Trade uses a lot of household behavioural elasticities in terms of consumption, production, import... but, since these are not available for WA, they were taken from the international literature without interrogating their relevance for WA.

- The study assumes that WA will not improve the recovery rate of the CDs which is far from 100%, a hypothesis contradicting the statement that "*the means of the PAPED will help improve the tax systems, limit the exemptions and fight corruption*".

[87] Peter Lunenborg, *Analysis of the West Africa EPA*, revised version of 2016, South Centre, Geneva.

6.3 – Other weaknesses in the methodology used by DG Trade

6.3.1 – DG Trade does not take into account the population increase in WA

What is most surprising is that the losses of CDs do not take into account the 64.4% increase in the WA population from 2015 to 2035 (when the EPAs liberalisation will be completed) insofar as it is claimed that this method does not need to do so, since it compares the impact with and without EPAs at the end of the period, during which WA would continue to tax its imports from the EU but would have to pay CDs on its exports to the same.

Because the basic situation without EPAs is not like the current one of non-reciprocal preferences since the Lomé agreements (1975) and even since independence, including for CI and Ghana insofar as both countries initialed iEPAs in 2007 and 2008 and have benefited from the Council Regulation No. 1528/2007 of 20 December 2007 (known as the market access regulation "MAR") which anticipated to apply to them the provisions for finalised EPAs. No, the basic situation is that without EPAs, where non-LDC developing countries have to pay the GSP CDs (or MFN CDs on bananas, hides and skins, and aluminum), which has been the actual situation for Nigeria simply because it had refused to initial an iEPA in 2008.

At least Lionel Fontagné of CEPII, author of another impact study of 2008 on the EPAs of SSA financed by DG Trade, told me that he did not take into account the population increase in his model of partial equilibrium based on the 2002-04 data and that he did not know whether DG Trade took it into account in its 2016 study[88]. It is unlikely that this has been done given that David Laborde of IFPRI participated in both studies.

Yet, explicitly taking into account the demographic change is all the more important as it will be very different in WA – where it would increase by 64% from 2015 to 2035, which would have a considerable impact on its import needs and export availabilities – and in the EU28 where the population is expected to stagnate and age and would even be overtaken by that of WA by 2030 according to the revised UN projections of 2017.

DG Trade writes that WA total imports, including from the rest of the world (RoW), would increase by 1.2% in 2035 with the EPA, of which 23.3% would come from the EU, compared with the situation without EPAs. It also estimates that WA's exports to the EU would increase by 4.1% with the EPA, which is hard to anticipate a priori (but we will come back to this) since, without EPAs, exports of CI and Ghana would be severely hampered by the CDs to pay to the EU and the loss of competitiveness with the other developing countries, especially those from Latin America with which the EU has concluded Free Trade Agreements (FTAs) giving them virtually the same benefits of duty-free imports (see below, especially for cocoa). Even with EPAs, the rise in exports to the EU would be hampered by the stagnation and ageing of the EU population and by the increased opportunities in the WA regional market resulting from its rising population.

[88] http://lionel.fontagne.free.fr/papers/fontalabmita_JAE.pdf

6.3.2 – We do not know the level of WA trade without EPAs in 2015

In its comparison of the evolution of the WA situation between 2015 and 2035 with and without EPAs, DG Trade considers that in 2015 the current preferential agreement would not have existed for CI and Ghana – in other words they would not have initialed iEPAs in 2007 and 2008 – so that since 2008, like Nigeria, they would have been in the much less favourable GSP regime, the other 13 WA States being in the LDCs EBA regime[89].

One can then wonder about the relevance of the figures kept by DG Trade – which are not published in the study, not even in the annexes which are very limited, as if DG Trade preferred not to expose itself to additional criticism – to characterise the economic situation of CI and Ghana in 2015, and in particular their foreign trade with the EU, the other WA countries and the rest of the world (RoW) since they had always benefited from preferential trade since their independence. It is therefore not possible to identify what would have been their trade since 2008 without this MAR regulation.

Hence it is likely that DG Trade simply considered that the actual trade of CI and Ghana in 2015 (presumably the beginning of the provisional application of the WA EPA) was the same as without the MAR regulation, whereas their exports to the EU-UK (taking into account the Brexit, even if it is not already effective) would have been much lower, since they accounted for 23.9% of the WA total exports to the EU28-UK and would have supported 94.7% of the GSP and MFN CDs to be paid by the 3 DCs

---

[89] Cape Verde was still a LDC in 2008 and joined the GSP+ regime in 2011 only, so that DG Trade erred is saying that it was in the GSP+ already in 2008.

(with Nigeria) and more generally by WA since the LDCs and Cape Verde were exempted[90]. This is casting a major question mark on the relevance of its study on WA EPA.

6.3.3 – Other DG Trade's significant errors on trade between the EU28 and WA

6.3.3.1 – Error on the balance of total trade between the EU and WA

DG Trade writes on page 2: "*In 2014, West Africa exported €37 billion worth of goods and imported goods of a value of €31 billion from the EU*" while in fact the € 37 bn are the CIF value of EU imports from WA, so that WA exports to the EU in FOB value were at least 20% lower. For WA imports from the EU, the opposite is true: the € 31 bn correspond to the EU FOB exports to WA for which the CIF value was at least 20% higher. However, later in the text (page 24), DG Trade rectified this mistake.

However, without criticising DG Trade, the EU recorded a surplus of € 4.7 bn in 2016 (exports of € 25.1 bn against imports of € 20.4 bn), which is due largely to the fall in oil prices and other raw materials exported by WA. In 2017, the EU28 surplus fell to € 3 bn due to higher imports (€ 24.9 bn) than exports (€ 28 bn).

This, however, undermines the DG Trade's argument that trade with the EU is already beneficial to WA without an EPA and that this can only improve with the EPA. This argument is all the less convincing that WA, except Nigeria which did not sign an iEPA, has always enjoyed

---

[90] *West Africa's losses of customs duties with and without the Economic Partnership Agreement (EPA) with the EU*, SOL, 7 February 2017, https://www.sol-asso.fr/wp-content/uploads/2017/01/West-Africas-losses-of-customs-duties-with-and-without-the-EPA-SOL-February-7-2017.pdf

duty free-quota free access to the EU market since 1995 and we do not see how the liberalisation of the WA market to EU exports could increase WA exports to the EU. As for Nigeria, most of its exports to the EU are not taxed.

6.3.3.2 – <u>Error on the cereals and beef trade between WA and the EU</u>

DG Trade writes: "*Almost all sectors in West Africa are expected to benefit from the EPAs through an increase in exports – with the highest increases in the following sectors: cereals (10.2%), other food (9.9%), red meat (8.4%) and wearing apparel (12.8%)*".

This is totally absurd for cereals and red meat since cereals are the main agricultural imports of WA – and even the second largest item of imports after fuels – and increased by 7.1 Mt in 2000 to 16.1 Mt in 2013 (increase of 6.1% per year), from 3.9 Mt to 7.4 Mt for wheat (4.4% per year). Of this total, the volume of cereals exported by the EU28 (including those incorporated in processed cereal products) was of 3.6 Mt in 2015, 3.4 Mt in 2016 and 2.9 Mt in 2017. DG trade shares the same ignorance for red meat as the EU did not import a single kg of beef and preparations from WA in 2015, but instead exported 93,100 tonnes; the EU imported just 22 tonnes in 2016 when it exported 97,844 tonnes and imported nothing again in 2017 but exported 102,980 tonnes. This ignorance of DG Trade on the reality of WA agriculture, which is its main productive sector, tells a lot about the reliability of its entire study of March 2016.

6.3.3.3 – <u>Error on the exclusion of milk powder and cereals in the EPA</u>

DG Trade argues that EPAs should not have a negative impact on ACP agriculture since they can prioritise agricultural products in the 20% of imports excluded from liberalisation. But several RECs (regional economic communities) negotiating EPAs, including ECOWAS, have chosen to protect a minimum of infant industries, forcing them to liberalise some basic food products. In particular 37.5% of WA agricultural imports would be liberalised for € 1.469 bn in EU FOB value in 2015, of which 80.4% taxed at 5% (Group A) would be liberalised from the beginning of liberalization in year T5; 17.1% taxed at 10% (group B) would be fully liberalised in T10 and 2.5% taxed at 20% (group C) would be fully liberalised in T20. However, EU28 exported 3,582 Mt of cereals to WA in 2015, of which 0,902 Mt included in processed cereal products with an FOB value of € 7.268 bn and an FOB price of 202.9 €/t. Similarly, the EU exported 2.5 Mt of dairy products in milk equivalent in 2016, for € 810 M[91].

It is clear that the reduction from 5% to 0 of the CD on cereals excluding rice (but the EU does not export rice) and on milk powder – which accounted for 84% of EU exports in milk equivalent (2.1 Mt over 2.4 Mt) – will have considerable consequences for the impoverishment of traditional cereal producers (millet, maize, sorghum, fonio), tubers (cassava, yams, taro) and plantains, on the one hand, and on the producers of animal products on the other hand. And this reduction will already begin on 3 September 2018 for the CI iEPA and on 15 December 2021 for the Ghana iEPA, while the WA EPA will not be finalised.

---

[91] We have shown in section 2.2.3 above that Eurostat has not yet identified a specific trade code for the fat-filled milk powder, FFMP), so that we have been reduced to make estimates.

6.3.3.4 – Error on the impact of the EPA on WA clothing exports to the EU

It is far from certain that the exports of clothing (Chapters 61 and 62 of the Harmonised System) from WA to the EU would increase with the EPA since the rules of origin (ROs), although improved with the EPAs compared to GSP or EBA for LDCs, are already into force for CI and Ghana EPAs, but the proportion of EU28 imports from CI and Ghana compared to its exports to these two countries fell from 3.1% in 2010 to 1.6% in 2015 and 2.3% in 2016.

DG Trade makes a mistake when it writes that "*The textile sector will benefit from preferential rules of origin (only a single transformation required in order to keep the benefit of the preferential access to the EU market) that other competing countries do not have, thus incentivising investment location and production in West Africa in line with West Africa's industrialisation strategies*".

In fact, the ROs of the African Growth Opportunity Act (AGOA) on clothing are much more favourable than those of the EU for SSA countries, even for those of relatively high GDP per capita (even Mauritius benefits from them because they can buy fabrics anywhere in the world ("third country fabric") while enjoying the status of original product to be exported to the US[92]. This had already tripled SSA exports to the US from 2000 to

[92] https://www.gao.gov/assets/680/671862.pdf; https://shenglufashion.wordpress.com/2016/04/28/african-growth-and-oppertunity-act-and-textile-apparel/; https://agoa.info/news/article/15264-us-raises-annual-agoa-quota-for-qualifying-textiles.html; http://web.ita.doc.gov/tacgi/eamain.nsf/d511529a12d016de852573930057380b/1e85488eb01fd2fd852573940049047d?OpenDocument

2005[93]. On the other hand, although improved with respect to ROs for LDCs, the EPA regime allows cumulation only for other inputs (yarn, fabrics) from either the EU (and Overseas Territories) or other ACP countries[94].

The best evidence of the superiority of US ROs is given by the fact that clothing exports from SSA to the US increased 4.7 times from 2010 to 2016 and by only 1.7 times to the EU and those to the US has exceeded those to the EU since 2015[95]. And USAID is very active in WA to support the textile industries and promote exports to the US[96].

During the debate of the INTA (International) Committee of the European Parliament on the possible ratification of Ghana iEPA, the head of the EPAs Division at DG Trade, Sandra Gallina, said that Ghana has been able to increase its exports of textile products by € 50 M[97]. We do not know where this figure comes from since exports of these products (for the three chapters 61 to 63 of the HS) from Ghana to the EU28 are almost non-existent, with €152,129 in 2015 against imports of € 93.9 M from the EU28, and € 536,000 exports to the United States.

---

93 http://unctad.org/en/Docs/itcdtab40_en.pdf

94 http://trade.ec.europa.eu/doclib/docs/2013/july/tradoc_151649.pdf

95 https://dataweb.usitc.gov/scripts/prepro.asp; https://www.watradehub.com/wp-content/uploads/2017/11/WATradeHub_FY17-Annual-Report_11062017.pdf

96 https://agoa.info/news/article/15300-ghana-garments-industry-receives-10-million-ghana-exim-support.html; https://www.watradehub.com/en/

97 *Comments after the INTA Committee's debate on Ghana's interim EPA*, SOL, October 17, 2016, https://www.sol-asso.fr/wp-content/uploads/2016/06/Comments-after-the-INTA-Committees-debate-on-Ghanas-interim-EPA-SOL18-October-2016.docx.pdf

6.3.3.5 – <u>Error on the impact of the EPA on cocoa products exported to the EU</u>

DG Trade stresses that, without EPAs, the processed cocoa exports of the three non LDCs countries would be subject to GSP CDs of 6.1% for cocoa paste, 4.2% for cocoa butter and 2.8% for cocoa powder. But DG Trade was careful not to write that since the FTAs passed in 2012 with 9 Latin American countries, the latter also export duty free all these products to the EU.

Even though, for chocolate per se (code 1806), on 3 TLs out of 23 for which the proportion of sugar exceeds 65%, the 9 Latin American countries will have to pay CDs of 7.6% plus CDs on the other incorporated agricultural products (dairy, cereals and sugar), but these 3 TLs accounted for only 16.4% of EU28 chocolate imports from these countries. However, EU28 imports of chocolate from Latin America remained very low (529 tonnes in 2016) compared to those coming from WA (32,038 tonnes) which themselves represent only 20.8% of total imports of the EU (154,223 tonnes), and also the CIF prices of chocolate coming from WA are much lower than those of Latin America and of the EU28 average CIF price, undoubtedly due to the difference in qualities.

In addition, the CETA agreement allows the EU to import from Canada all processed cocoa, including chocolate (code 1806), except for the two tariff lines that CI and Ghana do not export.

But the most formidable competitor for chocolate is Switzerland, the main supplier for the EU (67,131 tonnes) since all its exports to the EU are duty free. However, as Switzerland exports very fine chocolates, their average EU CIF price is twice that of WA (7,012 €/t against 3,535 €/t) and 67% higher than that of all EU imports (4,201 €/t).

6.3.3.6 – The EU might know something about the low price of cotton on the world market penalising West Africa

DG Trade writes in its box on the EU aid to CI cotton that "*The EPA will both facilitate producers' access to cheaper inputs and protect the country's cotton and textile industry from competing EU imports*". It is unclear as to how to interpret '*competing EU imports*'. What is known, however, is that 23,633 tonnes of cotton fibre (HS Code 5201), or 20% of the 178,110 tonnes imported by the EU in 2016 came from WA, of which 7,520 tonnes from CI, or 6.4% of the total from CI. But what is unknown is that the EU is heavily involved in lowering the world price of cotton due to its high level of dumping.

Indeed, EU subsidies were of € 799 M in 2016 – of which the EU notifies only one-third to the WTO, in the blue box, because 2/3 are hidden in the decoupled aid notified in the green box – for a production of 275,555 tonnes and an export of 271,841 tonnes, more than those of Mali, the largest exporter in SSA, owing to a subsidy of € 2,900/t, by far the highest in the world. Which, for an FOB export price of 1,457 €/t, gives a dumping rate of 199% against 22.3% for that of the US. While exports from the EU28 accounted for only 11.2% of those of the US (2.469 Mt)[98] and 3% of world exports, their total export subsidies were identical at € 800 M, which implies that the EU is co-responsible with the US for the suppression of the world price of cotton that affects SSA countries, of which CI.

The EU congratulates itself about its assistance through the 'Support Programme for the Consolidation of the

[98] *SOL's alternative methodology to the IATP assessment of US dumping*, January 1, 2018, https://www.sol-asso.fr/analyses-politiques-agricoles-jacques-b-2/

Framework for Action of the EU-Africa Partnership on Cotton', which would have amounted to € 651 M from 2004 to 2016[99], or € 54.3 M per year. But it is cautious not to compare it to the € 635 M of annual subsidies to its cotton exports granted on average over the same period, which is 11.7 times more!

6.3.3.7 – <u>The impact of the EPA on WA mango exports</u>

Even though the DG Trade Mango box (in its study) focuses on EU assistance to Senegal for phytosanitary protection, it begins by pointing out that the EU is importing them duty free-quota free (DFQF) as if non-LDC developing countries should pay CDs. But this is false since all EU imports of fresh, dried or processed mangoes are also DFQF from all countries. Similarly, shelled cashew exports, which all WA countries are seeking to increase, benefit from zero MFN duty. Therefore, this cannot be used as an argument to promote EPAs.

6.3.4 – The EU has hidden to West Africa the strong erosion of its preferences

The proliferation of recently concluded, or to be concluded, EU Free Trade Agreements (FTAs) with most developed and emerging countries will considerably erode the preferences of WA DFQF exports, which are supposed to be sustained by the EPA and iEPAs.

WA exports to the EU will experience a significant decline in competitiveness vis-à-vis the 9 Andean and Central American countries that have implemented FTAs

---

[99] http://www.rtb.bf/2017/03/partenariat-ue-afrique-sur-le-coton-fin-du-programme-dappui-a-la-consolidation-du-cadre-daction-sur-fond-dactivites-de-promotion-du-coton/

with the EU28 since 2012 (2015 for Ecuador) because they can also export DFQF all agricultural and fishery products, except for bananas for which the CDs are gradually decreasing to 75 €/t from 2020 whereas, without WA EPA or iEPA, non-LDC ACP countries will have to pay the full MFN duty (reduced from 127 €/t to 117 €/t since 1 January 2018). As regards chocolate, the 9 Latin American countries will have to pay specific duty only, but not the ad valorem duty.

In addition, Article 8 of Regulation 978/2012 of 25 October 2012 stipulates that MFN CD will be applied when EU imports under an HS chapter exceed 17.5% of its total imports from GSP countries for three years. The Commission had already adopted an EU Regulation 2016/330 of 8 March 2016 for imports of Chapter 06 of the HS (Seed and Cut Flower) of Kenya[100]. This should also be the case for CI cocoa products which accounted for 38.1% of total EU28 cocoa imports from 2013 to 2015, as well as for Ghana which accounted for 19.2% of total imports. However, as far as we know, DG Trade does not seem to have made such a regulation for CI and Ghana cocoa to encourage them to ratify their iEPAs.

But this regulation only applies to GSP countries and not those that have signed FTAs with the EU, such as Ecuador, which nevertheless accounted for 27.7% of bananas imported by the EU28 from 2013 to 2015 in volume terms, and 25.3% in value. A fortiori these percentages would be much higher if one referred to the imports coming from the GSP beneficiary countries. Compared to FTAs, GSP should rather be understood as being "Generalised System of Penalties"! Yet the per capita gross national income was of $ 6,010 in Ecuador in

---

[100] http://trade.ec.europa.eu/doclib/docs/2016/march/tradoc_154349.pdf

2015 compared to $ 1,410 in CI, $ 1,480 in Ghana and $ 1,380 in Kenya[101]. Fortunately, Article 8 does not apply to GSP+ beneficiary countries, which would make it a good alternative to the EPA[102]. That is probably the reason why DG Trade did not want to encourage them to apply for GSP+ since it does not want to grant it to Nigeria as that would bury the WA EPA.

Moreover, the political scandal is that the reduced or zero CD on imports from the countries that have signed FTAs means that the EU does not care if they comply with the fundamental international conventions on human rights, social rights, environment and good governance, which it demands from ACP countries to grant them the GSP+ status. According to the 2016 Human Rights Watch report, "*Rampant crime and impunity for human rights abuses remain the norm in Honduras. Despite a downward trend in recent years, the murder rate is among the highest in the world*"[103]; "*Violence and extortion by powerful criminal organisations remain serious problems in Guatemala. Corruption within the justice system, combined with intimidation against judges and prosecutors, contributes to high levels of impunity. Gang-related violence is also one of the principal factors prompting people, including unaccompanied youth, to leave the country*".

Even though a peace agreement was recently concluded between the Colombian government and the FARC, at the time of the signing of the EU FTA in 2012 the country

---

[101] http://data.worldbank.org/indicator/NY.GNP.PCAP.CD

[102] http://www.ictsd.org/bridges-news/eclairage-sur-les-n%C3%A9gociations/news/entretien-exclusif-avec-le-commissaire-europ%C3%A9en-au

[103] https://www.hrw.org/sites/default/files/world_report_download/wr2016_web.pdf

was not a good example in terms of human rights. This situation continues to obtain as "*Human rights defenders, trade unionists, journalists, indigenous and Afro-Colombian leaders, and other community activists face death threats and violence, but perpetrators are rarely held accountable*".

According to the 2015-16 Amnesty International Report, "*Levels of gang-related violence and organised crime in El Salvador surged and homicide rates soared. According to official records, 4,253 homicides were registered in the first eight months of the year, compared with 3,912 for the whole of 2014. Criminal violence forced many Salvadorians to leave the country, and also led to the internal displacement of thousands of families, according to the Civil Society Roundtable against Forced Displacement Provoked by Violence and Organised Crime*"[104].

Even EU banana producers, from the Canary Islands, suffer from loss of competitiveness vis-à-vis Latin American producers who have signed FTAs with the EU: "*The main problem is the non-compliance with the standards of environmental protection, food safety and social and labour protection for Europe, which are required for European productions, but are not required or controlled in the case of third countries*"[105].

In the CETA FTA with Canada, provisionally applied since 21 September 2017, the EU has immediately liberalised almost all TLs for which CI, Ghana, Nigeria and Kenya are due to pay MFN, GSP or GSP+ CDs without EPAs. The EU offer allows duty-free imports

---

[104] https://www.amnesty.org/download/Documents/POL1025522016ENGLISH.PDF

[105] http://www.freshplaza.com/article/166776/European-bananas-threatened-by-Ecuador-EU-agreement

from Canada on all processed cocoa (including chocolate, except for 2 tariff lines that CI does not export), on all canned tuna exported by CI and Ghana (some TLs are liberalised only in year 8, but do not include those imported by the EU from CI and Ghana), on all chapter 06 (including cut flowers) and all vegetables exported by Kenya to the EU (including fresh beans), on cereal soups and bran, hides and skins (Chapter 41) and aluminum (Chapter 76), both products on which the EU applies MFNs, including on GSP+ regime. In fact, the EU tariff offer to Canada liberalises all industrial products immediately, with the exception of Chapter 87 (automobiles) where liberalisation will extend over 3, 5 or 7 years.

Other arguments on the loss of competitiveness of agricultural exports from WA to the EU were presented in a 2015 paper[106].

6.3.5 – The MFN clause could also work against the EU in favour of CI and Ghana

The problem of erosions of preferences for the ACP countries that have signed EPAs must be compared with the MFN clause. While it is generally believed that this penalises only the ACP countries which are obliged to grant to the EU the more advantageous treatment they would grant to other developed or emerging countries, – a major aspect that will be discussed at length in section 7.2.3 – it could also work against the EU. Let us consider

[106] *The false argument of the GSP duties that the exporters of Ivory Coast, Ghana and Nigeria would have to pay to the EU without the EPA*, SOL, April 12, 2015: https://www.sol-asso.fr/wp-content/uploads/2015/04/Le_faux_argument_des_droits_de_douane_du_SPG_a_payer_en_l_absence_d_APE_12_avril_20154.pdf

the clause for the WA EPA and for the iEPAs of CI and Ghana.

Article 16 of the WA EPA provides: "*MFN Clause 1) The Parties reaffirm their commitment with regard to the Enabling Clause 2) The European Union Party shall grant the West Africa Party any more favourable tariff treatment that it grants to a third Party if the European Union Party becomes party to a preferential agreement with the third Party in question after the signing of this Agreement*".

It has to be said that the clause does not apply to the WA EPA since it has not yet been signed by all countries. Nevertheless, one of the obstacles to Nigeria's signing of the EPA is the prospect of a lack of competitiveness, especially for its hides and skins exports which are subject to the MFN CD of 6.50%, while those of Canada are duty free since September 2017. One of the arguments that also played a role in the ratification of Ghana iEPA was that its exports of aluminum would have been subject to the MFN CD of 3%, even under the GSP+ scheme.

More broadly, the Enabling Clause, under which the EPAs have been concluded, provides in Article 5 that "*The developed countries do not expect the developing countries, in the course of trade negotiations, to make contributions which are inconsistent with their individual development, financial and trade needs*". Which, in accordance with the WTO Appellate Body's interpretation of India's prosecution of the EU's preferential regime to countries fighting against drug trafficking (precursor of the GSP+), is possible and desirable to differentiate preferences among developing countries according to their level of development. In this case the EU with its FTAs operates backward preferences to the detriment of ACP countries.

But let's look at the case of CI and Ghana iEPAs, which have been applied since the end of 2016, before the EU

CETA FTA with Canada. Article 17, paragraph 1, of CI and Ghana iEPAs states that "*The EC* [European Commission] *Party shall grant the Ivorian Party any more favourable treatment applicable as a result of the European Community becoming party to a free trade agreement with third parties after signing this Agreement*". One might think that, since CI and Ghana's EPAs have had full access (DFQF) to the EU market since the end of 2016 (excluding arms), later FTAs with other third countries, including CETA with Canada, cannot be more favourable. But the expression 'any more favourable treatment' can be understood more broadly than the only advantages of access to the EU market and should rather focus on the protection of the WA market and its Member States, particularly CI and Ghana. As a result, Canada does not face all the non-trade constraints imposed on ACP EPA signatories.

For example in the area of agricultural subsidies, while the WA EPA states in paragraph 6 of Article 48 that "*The European Union Party undertakes to refrain from the use of export subsidies for agricultural products exported to West Africa*", this provision is absent from the iEPAs of CI and Ghana. In the CETA Agreement, Article 4 of Chapter 9 deals with agricultural and fisheries subsidies, while Article 5 deals with agricultural and export fisheries subsidies, which implies that Article 4 deals with domestic subsidies, which allows for the opening of consultations: "*If a Party considers that a subsidy, or the provision of government support, granted by the other Party, is adversely affecting, or may adversely affect, its interests with respect to agricultural goods or fisheries products, it may express its concerns to the other Party and request consultations on the matter*".

While this does not imply immediate prosecutions by the CI and Ghana against the EU, it allows at least a thorough exchange of arguments on their impact. It is therefore a provision that the CI and Ghana can claim as a 'more favourable treatment' that the EU must grant to their iEPAs. Thus EU28 cereals exports to CI received € 42 M in subsidies in 2016 and € 11.7 M in dairy products. Similarly EU cereals exports to Ghana received € 7.1 M in subsidies and dairy products € 12.8 M, and € 11.9 M can be added to poultry meat (which the CI protects efficiently). As for Nigeria, the EU subsidies on cereals were of € 47.6 M and those on dairy products of € 27.9 M.

6.3.6 – Criticisms on the final conclusions of the DG Trade study

It should be recalled that DG Trade clearly announces that "*In a conservative manner, only the impact of the tariff reductions was assessed, i.e. what is easily quantifiable from the agreement. Essential provisions of the EPA (rules of origin, trade facilitation, cooperation on norms, the EPA Development Programme, etc.) were left out from the model since they are difficult to quantify without making strong assumptions; still they weigh in favour of West African countries*".

Despite this statement that "*only the impact of tariff reductions was assessed*", we must simply understand that "*As a result of tariff reductions, collected import duties will on average be lower in 2035 (by 11.7%)*" with EPA than without EPA. That is insufficient information since we do not know the amounts of the tariff cuts in € M, whether it is more with or without EPA, and whether it will be more in 2035 than at the start of the regional EPA in 2015. None of these amounts is included in the appendices, which are very limited.

In a presentation on the state of play of the EPA negotiations to the European Parliamentarians of the INTA (International) and DROI (Human Rights)

Committees on 15 October 2015, the Head of these negotiations at DG Trade, Sandra Gallina, told them: "*Some critics of the EPAs mention the loss of fiscal resources that will be brought about by the liberalisation of tariff lines. On the one hand these losses are difficult to assess, on the other hand it must be borne in mind that it will be in reality a simple transfer between the funds of the ACP States and the pockets of the ACP consumers who will be winners*"[107].

Who does not see the contradiction between the assertion of the study that "*the impact of tariff cuts... is easily quantifiable*" and that of Sandra Gallina that "*these losses are difficult to assess*", hence surely the decision to remain vague by only giving a percentage of the reduction of CDs.

Moreover, DG Trade would surely have a hard time giving the amount of CDs collected in 2015 without the EPA as CI and Ghana would have been in the GSP regime (and MFN for bananas and aluminum) since 2008, like Nigeria. These two countries would have therefore already lost much of their competitiveness by having had to pay significant CDs on their exports of bananas, pineapples, processed cocoa, canned tuna and aluminum to the EU since 2008, and their export earnings would have weakened considerably. As a result, their imports from the EU would also have been much lower than under the effective MAR regime that prevailed in 2015 and to-date, and the CDs collected on these declining EU imports would have also been weaker.

On the other hand, the continuation of the GSP and MFN regime until 2035 would continue to reduce the competitiveness of the exports of CI and Ghana on the EU

---

[107] Informal report of an European Parliamentary assistant having participated to this debate.

market – competitiveness already weakened by the EU FTAs with the Latin American countries and Vietnam, and even more so with the FTAs still to be concluded, notably with Mercosur, Chile, Mexico, the Philippines, India and others – and therefore the GSP and MFN to be paid to the EU on these exports would also be much lower. As noted earlier, these two countries would have supported 94.7% of the GSP and MFN CDs to be paid by WA since LDCs and Cape Verde (which was still an LDC in 2008) are exempted. Hence it is in one's best interest not finalise the regional EPA and denounce the iEPAs.

Hence the interest of not finalizing the regional EPA and denouncing the IEPAs since the decrease in customs revenue on imports from the EU with WA EPA would have started in 2020 if the EPA had started to be applied in 2015. It should have started on February 3, 2017 for the iEPA of CI for some TLs and at the latest on September 3, 2018 for many TLs.

The main conclusions of the DG Trade study are as follows: " *Twenty years after the entry into force, the tariff reductions have a small but positive impact on both real GDP and economic welfare for all West African countries. For example, in 2035, Côte d'Ivoire's real GDP will be 0.5% higher and welfare 0.7% higher, compared to the situation where an EPA would not be in place... It is worth recalling that this change in tariff revenue, which would be equivalent to 2% of total government revenues, is merely a displacement of resources from governments to consumers and companies*".

Indeed, the fall in domestic prices linked to non-LDCs' imports from the EU could increase consumers' 'welfare' in the short run if this fall in prices is transmitted to them, which is rarely the case, but this 'welfare' will drop sharply for all those whose incomes will fall as a result of job losses related to the loss of competitiveness of regional companies and businesses, particularly for the 90% of the population in the informal sector, 60% of which are working in tiny family farms.

But the percentages of the difference reflected in the GDP and 'welfare' with and without EPA after 20 years are so minimal that they are absolutely not significant and reliable, considering the multiple flaws of the model. At least DG Trade agrees that "*Estimating the future effects of trade agreements is not an exact science, even when the content of the agreement is known*".

Suffice to say that the DG Trade study as well as the model that accompanies it were manufactured in a way to show a positive impact and provide decision-makers with a semblance of scientific guarantee.

VII - A Realistic Methodology on the Impacts of the WA EPA and CI and Ghana iEPAs

The extent of the shortcomings and shortfalls in the methodology used by DG Trade, in particular its Computable General Equilibrium Model (CGEM) to assess the impact of the WA EPA and of other World Bank studies on the impact of the WA EPA on Ghana and Nigeria, justifies the use of another method.

One of the important arguments, though more political than economic, made by all the studies using CGEM is that only this type of model can calculate and demonstrate that EPAs will not have a negative impact on the rest of the world (RoW). In this regard, the DG Trade study concludes that "*Total exports from West Africa to the world are positively affected by the EPA and so are total imports, though to a smaller extent. West African exports are expected to increase on average by 1.5% and imports by 1.2%*". Yet, the IFPRI study published three months earlier and prepared by the same expert, David Laborde, concluded that "*The gains in terms of access to foreign markets are limited or nil for West African countries, especially West African LDCs*".

To overcome these contradictions and the lack of reliable data in the DG Trade study, another methodology based on actual trade figures is necessary, even if one has to resort to some assumptions on the evolution from 2015 to 2035 which are clearly announced and can be modified. This does not preclude calculating the impact on customs revenue of trade with the RoW. The adopted methodology will make it possible to clearly calculate the CDs to be paid by the 3 DCs on their exports to the EU – rather to the EU28-UK because the Brexit should be taken into account in the future – in the absence of an EPA that DG Trade does not highlight since it merely announces a percentage of losses with the EPA.

This general methodology for the WA EPA will be complemented by that appropriate for the iEPAs of CI and Ghana.

7.1 – Evaluation of Customs Revenue Losses

7.1.1 – The basic situation in which the EPA impact is compared is in T (2015) under the MAR regime

SOL estimates the loss of customs revenues (CRs: CDs plus VAT on imports) by comparing the current situation (T in 2015) where WA taxes its imports from the EU28-UK – because it is necessary to take the Brexit into account in the future – and where its exports to the EU are not taxed – except for those of Nigeria that has not signed an iEPA – until the beginning of liberalisation (in T5) where the losses of CRs begin for all WA States, even if the VAT gains on increased imports from the EU exceed the CDs losses on these imports during the first years.

By considering, as DG Trade does, that the base without EPAs is the one where the exports of the three DCs of WA – CI, Ghana and Nigeria – pay the GSP or MFN CDs, we realise that this leads to an indetermination of the amount of trade (exports and imports) in 2015 since the three DCs would have been in the GSP and MFN regime since 2008. Then the CRs losses are based on the next following steps.

7.1.2 – Steps in the assessment of the customs revenue losses in the WA EPA

The steps below are a summary of the SOL study "West African Customs Losses with and without EPAs" of February 13, 2018[108].

1) Since WA customs statistics on imports are unreliable and published after very long delays and those of Comtrade and TradeMap limited to 6-digit HS codes and not always reliable either[109], we will use Eurostat data on EU FOB exports where TLs are at 10 digits – as those of the WA CET and CI iEPA –, which are converted into WA CIF values by estimating that the FOB-to-CAF differential is 20% on average for the entire WA, which is probably a very conservative estimate. This average takes into account a smaller gap in Senegal than in landlocked Sahelian countries or more remote countries such as Nigeria, where delays in ship unloading lead to additional costs (surestaries).

However, unlike the studies published by ITAQA, IFPRI and DG Trade, which use guesswork to assess the percentage of CRs collected because the official CET and VAT are not implemented at 100%, we assume that it will be in the future even if presently there are a lot of legal exemptions, multiple unlawful ransoms by the police, the army or the so-called 'understanding' with customs

---

[108] *West Africa's losses of customs duties with and without the Economic Partnership Agreement (EPA) with the EU*, SOL, 7 February 2017, https://www.sol-asso.fr/wp-content/uploads/2017/01/West-Africas-losses-of-customs-duties-with-and-without-the-EPA-SOL-February-7-2017.pdf

[109] For example, according to Trade Map, ECOWAS CIF (costs, insurance, freight) imports from EU28 are 8.8% lower in 2015 than EU28 FOB (free on board) exports to ECOWAS, which should be the opposite.

officers, or even the double charging by some Sahelian countries of CDs on products already cleared at coastal ports. Extending this underestimation of CDs up to T20 suggests that WA is doomed to not improving its practices whereas DG Trade claims that the EPA will contribute to it.

2) The WA EPA liberalisation schedule is established for 4 groups of products – groups A, B and C for those liberalised from T5 – whose CDs reduction rates are 0%, 5%, 10% or 20% –, and group D for those excluded from liberalisation, taxed at 35% (D3), 20% (D2), 10% or 0% (D1). Imports of products in this group are not prohibited but their CDs are not reduced with the EPA.

After a very long calculation process, TL by TL for the 97 chapters of the CET, a summary table is drawn up in the annex with, in rows, the groups from A to D (with their subgroups) and, in columns, the FOB value of EU exports, the CDs and their average rate in T, and the 4 columns on CDs in T5, T10, T15 and T20, given the liberalisation of products in groups A, B and C.

3) Recalculation is made of the value of imports and CDs after the conversion from FOB EU to CAF WA.

4) Recalculation is made of these values to take population growth into account. Taking into consideration the United Nations average prospects from 2015 to 2050, we can deduce the population growth rates from T (2015) to T5 (2020), from T5 to T10 (2025), from T10 to T15 (2030), from T15 to T20 (2035) and from T20 to T35 (2050). We note that imports grew about twice as fast as the population from 2000 to 2015 (5.77% against 2.75%) but, as a conservative measure, we expect for the future a growth rate of imports equal to that of the gradually declining population growth.

5) As for the trade diversion affecting imports of the liberalised products of groups A, B and C, after reading

several studies, we cautiously limit ourselves to a diversion percentage of 20% and deduct the CDs losses (at an average rate of 8.59% in 2015) from T5 to T20 (and even T35) on these diverted imports.

6) The next step is the calculation of VAT on imports of liberalised and excluded products, given that it corresponds to 16% of the sum of imports (after diversion) plus the CDs.

7) The next step is the calculation of CDs and VAT on imports from EU28-UK without EPA. In this case, there is no longer any need to distinguish the CDs according to the liberalised and excluded groups of products and the average CD of 10.73% observed in 2015 is applied to all WA imports from the EU28-UK. This results in a loss of € 3.4 bn in 2035 and a cumulative loss of € 28.4 bn related to the 76.2% liberalised imports from the EU28-UK.

8) CDs and VAT are then calculated on imports not affected by trade diversion – those coming from WA (on which there is no CD but only VAT) and from the RoW – and whose CD rates per group are unchanged from T (2015). The €31.3 bn CIF imports of WA from the EU28-UK in 2015 accounted for 34.2% of total WA imports, which represented € 91.4 bn, of which € 9.9 bn (10.8%) from WA and € 50.3 bn (55%) from the RoW, of which € 3.3 bn (3.6%) from the UK. We distribute WA imports from intra-WA and RoW in proportion to their relative shares in total WA imports: 16.42% from WA and 83.58% from the RoW. But we must subtract the CRs related to the 20% trade diversion in favour of more imports from the EU28-UK, starting at € 466 M in T5, which is divided between intra-WA imports and imports from the RoW according to their relative shares in the total imports of WA.

9) Finally, the net CRs on WA imports from intra-WA and ROW increased from € 16.7 bn in T5 to € 24 bn in T20.

These revenues are added to those on imports from the EU28-UK without EPAs – which rise from € 26.8 bn in T5 to € 38.6 bn in T20 – and are compared with the net losses of CRs on imports from the EU28-UK with the EPA, by calculating the ratio of these losses to total revenues without EPAs. The ratio of net CRs losses on EPA-related imports from the EU28-UK to total revenue of all origins without EPAs would increase from 7.9% in T5 to 18.1% in T20.

Trade diversion in favour of imports from the EU28-UK results in a 7.9% decrease in trade from both the RoW and WA throughout the period, showing that this methodology allows to better calculate the impact of the EPA on trade with the RoW than the DG Trade methodology, which concludes that there is an increase in imports from the RoW.

7.1.3 – The GSP and MFN CDs to be paid on WA DCs exports to the EU

In order to put pressure on the other WA States to sign the WA EPA, CI and Ghana have overestimated the GSP and MFN CDs to pay on their exports to the EU, and Kenya has made similar pressure on the 4 other EAC States by overestimating its CDs to pay on cut flowers and beans. But DG Trade has been careful not to give figures on these CDs to be paid to the EU, even if it has necessarily taken them into account to conclude that WA is better off with the EPA than without.

7.1.4 – Methodology to assess the CD losses in CI and Ghana iEPAs

This assessment is made in the present context, confirmed on 9 April 2018 by President Buhari, who said that Nigeria would not sign the WA EPA, which will be buried while CI and Ghana iEPAs will become permanent. However we will not yet consider the impact of the signing of the Continental Free Trade Area (AfCFTA), which will be discussed further below. Without the WA EPA the losses of CDs and VAT of CI and Ghana on their imports from the EU28-UK would be lower since the CDs of their iEPAs are lower, although not always on some TLs of CI. On the other hand, it is very likely that the other WA States will tax their imports from CI and Ghana so as not to be invaded by the products that these countries would have liberalised while they themselves, particularly the 12 LDCs, would continue to collect the CDs of the WA CET on their imports from the EU28-UK.

7.1.4.1 – <u>Customs revenue losses in Ghana iEPA</u>

The analysis below is a summary of the SOL study on "*Ghana should never have implemented its interim EPA*" of 13 February 2018[110].

The Ministry of Trade and Industry of Ghana (MOTI) had already grossly underestimated Ghana's losses of customs revenues (CRs) if the WA EPA is implemented, based on the impact assessment conducted by the World Bank and MOTI in January 2015 using 2013 data[111]. It

[110] https://www.sol-asso.fr/wp-content/uploads/2017/01/Le-Ghana-naurait-jamais-d%C3%BB-mettre-en-%C5%93uvre-son-APE-int%C3%A9rimaire-SOL-13-02-18.pdf. This file should be updated to take into account the specific and lower CDs of its iEPA compared to those of the WA CET, as we have done for the CI iEPA.

[111] MacLeod, Jamie; Von Uexkull, Jan Erik; Shui, Lulu, *Assessing the economic impact of the ECOWAS CET and economic partnership agreement on Ghana*, 1st January 2015, http://documents.worldbank.org/curated/en/845041467999971258/Assessing-the-economic-impact-of-the-ECOWAS-CET-and-economic-partnership-agreement-on-Ghana

estimated the percentage of the value of liberalised products at 65% for the EU28 while they were 75% in 2015 for the EU28-UK. Most importantly, this study is based on "*a simple assumption of 3 percent annual growth in all government revenue sources, using fiscal data from the 2013 International Monetary Fund (IMF) Article IV report as the base*", adding: "*As other revenue sources increase in importance, the relative reliance on import revenues and hence the noticeable impact of import revenue losses from the EPA will fall*". Moreover, the World Bank has made the same assumption in its assessment of the impact of WA EPA on Nigeria. It is then easy to deduce that the WA EPA would increase CRs in Ghana by 1.2% per year excluding the reform of the CET! Yet the last IMF report on Ghana in September 2017 is much less optimistic, with growth of 3.5% in 2016, the lowest in two decades[112], and the share of CRs in total tax revenue, far from having fallen, rose from 12.7% in 2015 to 15% in 2016 (excluding VAT on imports charged to indirect taxes).

According to the ActionAid Ghana's study of July 2013, the liberalisation of 75% of imports from the EU with the iEPA would lead to CRs losses of $ 1.127 bn from 2008 to 2022 (the last year of liberalisation) but, without the iEPA, these losses would be offset by the revenues on imports from the RoW, so that in 2022 CRs without iEPA would be $ 242 M compared to $ 70 M with iEPA. Still the study does not take the Brexit into account, which will reduce the revenue coming from the EU but increase those coming from the RoW.

Third World Network Africa, based in Accra, also points out that "*Today, more than 90 per cent of Ghana's*

[112] https://www.imf.org/en/News/Articles/2017/08/30/pr17337-ghana-imf-executive-board-completes-fourth-review-under-the-ecf

most dynamic manufacturing exports go to the West Africa sub-region... the EPAs directly undermine this"[113]. This finding was confirmed by the above World Bank study of 2015: "*The most important export market for employment is ECOWAS: exporters to ECOWAS employed 38.7 percent of the sample's workers. The second most important market was the European Union: exporters to the European Union employed 4.9 percent of the sample's workers*".

On the other hand, the perpetuation of the iEPA without the finalisation of the WA EPA will force Ghana to pay CDs on its exports to the rest of WA. These exports to WA were of € 1.213 bn in 2016 (Trade Map has no data for 2015) in Ghana FOB value, or 12.6% of its total exports of € 9.628 bn and 50.7% of its exports to the EU28-UK of €2.394 bn. The calculation of the CET CDs by 6-digit TL shows that Ghana should have paid € 165.9 M in CIF ECOWAS value in T (2017), implying an average CD of 11.9%. We limit ourselves to calculating the CDs on ECOWAS without taking Mauritania into account because the exports to this country were negligible at € 135,000.

The CDs to be paid on its exports to WA will not start until 2021 since its iEPA has been applied since 15 December 2016, even though Ghana has contradicted the status quo clause of the iEPA prohibiting to increase its applied CDs since it continues to use those of the WA CET. These losses would then increase in line with its population, from € 175 M in 2017 to € 189 M in 2020 and € 272 M in 2035, the cumulative losses increasing from € 728 M in 2020 to € 4.2 bn in 2035. The annual CDs to pay on Ghana's exports to ECOWAS with the EPA (of WA or

---

[113] http://www.socialwatch.org/node/13598

iEPA) would be 2.1 times higher in 2020 and 3.4 times higher in 2035 than those to be paid on Ghana's exports to U28-UK without EPAs. And the cumulative CDs would be 2.9 times higher in 2035 towards ECOWAS than towards EU28-UK.

If we add the CRs losses (CDs + VAT) on the liberalised imports from the EU28-UK – which would rise from € 185 M in T5 (2022) to € 1.440 bn in T20 (2037) – the total annual losses increase from € 575 M in T5 to € 759 M in T10, € 933.5 M in T15 and € 1.027 bn in T20.

However, the non-liberalised imports from WA and the RoW would generate significant CRs since, out of total imports of € 12.205 bn from Ghana in 2016, imports from the EU28-UK accounted for 26.41% (€ 3.223 bn), those from WA 12.49% (€ 1.525 bn) and those from the RoW 61.10% (€ 7.458 bn). Assuming that these imports would be taxed at the average rate of 11.05% calculated for 2015 on all products imported from EU28-UK, the CDs would be of € 824 M in T (there is no CDs on imports from WA) and the VAT of € 1.437 bn, for a total of € 2.261 bn which, given the population increase, would rise from € 2.315 bn in T to € 2.579 bn in T5 and € 3.388 bn in T20.

As a result, the total net CRs – after deducting the CRs losses on imports from the EU28-UK and those to be paid on exports to WA from the CRs collected on non-liberalized imports from WA and the RoW – would increase from € 2 bn in T5 to € 2,361 bn in T20. And the CRs losses related to the EPA and those to be paid on Ghana's exports to WA would represent 22.3% of the CRs collected on imports from WA in T5 and 30.3% in T20.

7.1.4.2 – CI losses in customs revenues with its iEPA

The analysis below is a summary of the SOL study of 31 March 2018[38] on "The absurd interim EPA of Côte d'Ivoire".

The calculation steps are the same as for WA EPA and Ghana iEPA, but CI iEPA is very specific as discussed in Section 2.2 above.

The annual losses in customs revenue (CRs: CDs + VAT) on imports from the EU28-UK rise from € 65 M in T5 (3 September 2021) to € 389 M in T21 (2036) and € 580 M in T51. Cumulative losses increase from € 65 M in T5 (2021) to € 4.423 bn in T20 (2036) and € 11.692 bn in T35 (2051). These losses are considerable, but lower than the CDs to be paid on CI exports to the rest of WA with the iEPA, but the two combined are much higher than the GSP and NPF CDs to be paid on CI exports to the EU28-UK without the iEPA.

The annual CDs to be paid on CI exports to the rest of the WA increase from € 382.3 M in 2020 to € 467.3 M in 2025, € 527.4 M in 2030, € 591.6 M in 2035 and € 816.1 M in 2050. The cumulated CDs would jump to € 9.160 bn in 2035 and € 19.729 bn in 2050. These cumulative losses in CDs would be added to the losses in CRs on imports from EU28-UK and would be 2.3 times higher in 2035.

In comparison with these CR losses due to the iEPA, the GSP and NPF CDs to be paid on CI exports to the EU28-UK in the absence of iEPA would rise from € 170 M in T (2015) to € 196 M in T5, € 275 M in T20 and € 375 M in T35. The cumulated CDs losses would jump to € 1.111 bn in T5, € 4.657 bn in T20 and € 9.540 bn in T35.

These cumulative losses of the GSP + MFN CDs to be paid to the EU28-UK without iEPA are certainly considerable but remain much lower than those due to the CDs to be paid on exports to WA with the iEPA, the more so when we add the CRs losses on imports from the

EU28-UK with the iEPA. The net cumulative losses would thus increase from € 786 M in 2021 to € 2.280 bn in 2025, € 5.153 bn in 2030, € 8.537 bn in 2035 and € 21.301 bn in 2050, and the conclusion is that CI should denounce its iEPA.

However, the decline in CRs on imports from the EU28-UK due to the iEPA should not obscure the fact that CI will continue to receive CRs on its imports from the rest of WA and the RoW, although its CRs will be reduced by trade diversions in favour of imports from EU28-UK.

With the iEPA, the CD diversion is estimated at € 673 M in T5 against € 411 M in the calculation carried out previously on the basis of the ECOWAS CET. There is no doubt that the regional disintegration caused by the implementation of CI (and Ghana) IEPA, and in particular the fact that the CI will have to pay CDs on its exports to the rest of WA, will also result in lower CI imports from the rest of WA.

This therefore implies that CI will get out of the ECOWAS CET and will find it difficult to continue using the CET in its imports from the RoW. It could then use the lower CDs of the iEPA without being forced to liberalise its imports from the RoW. This would be a big slap on the EU28-UK which would lose its competitiveness compared to CI imports from the RoW! Especially when the lower CD rates in the iEPA may not reduce total CRs from the RoW as trade diversion would be greatly reduced or even reversed to the detriment of the EU!

7.2 – Other non-financial constraints imposed on EPA signatories

The non-financial constraints imposed by the EU on EPA signatories will greatly reduce their space of political manoeuvre in many areas, including the rendez-vous clause, the standstill clause and the MFN clause, given, as already noted, the inequalities between WA and the EU in the use of safeguards.

7.2.1 – The rendez-vous clause

While Article 106 of the WA EPA provides that six months after the conclusion of the WA EPA, negotiations should *begin* to broaden the liberalisation of the EPA to new themes that all developing countries have refused at the WTO – on services, intellectual property, investment, competition, government procurement, current payments and capital movements, sustainable development, protection of personal data –, article 44 of the iEPA goes much faster since this extension must be *concluded as soon as possible*, i.e. from the end of 2008 or one year after the provisional application, even if this clause only applies to the WA EPA, which is illogical since CI would obviously not have been able to engage the entire WA in these negotiations even if the WA EPA would have been applied on a provisional basis. The same provision applies to Ghana's APEi.

7.2.2 – The status quo clause

This is the prohibition, common to all FTAs (Free Trade Agreements), to increase the CDs applied at the beginning of the provisional application of the WA EPA (Article 9) or CI iEPA (Article 15) and Ghana iEPA (Article 15) on imports from the EU. This provision is deeply unfair since, as a WTO member, EU28 has bound CDs enabling it to raise its applied CDs, even if they are in fact very close to the bound ones. It could reduce some applied CDs and raise them occasionally. Even if all ECOWAS States are WTO members and have bound

CDs, if ECOWAS takes steps to becoming a full WTO member as the EU in order to get bound CDs set at the average level of the bound CDs of its 15 Member States, weighted by the importance of their extra-ECOWAS imports, it is possible that the EU could be tempted to stop this application at the WTO to secure for itself the opening of the WA market.

As discussed in section 4.3, the EU benefits from much better bilateral and multilateral safeguards than WA, including CI and Ghana, which is a means for it to divert the standstill clause. It should be added that another very powerful way of diverting this clause is through its ability to continue dumping its agricultural exports through its huge domestic subsidies, decoupled or not, on its exports since it has refused to deal with this issue in the EPAs and to change the WTO rules. Yet subsidies have a strong import substitution effect, i.e. they have the same effect as CDs.

7.2.3 - The MFN clause

A major argument that should shake CI and Ghana is related to the consequences of having both implemented their iEPAs with the EU since the end of 2016 and signed the African Continental Free Trade Area (AfCFTA) at the Extraordinary Summit of the Heads of State of the African Union on 21 March 2018 in Kigali. It is the MFN (Most Favoured Nation) clause of their iEPAs that obliges them to extend to the EU the CD advantages granted to African States in the AfCFTA.

There are three very important differences in the terms of this clause between the WA EPA and the CI and Ghana's iEPAs.

According to Article 16 of the WA EPA "*The West Africa Party shall grant the European Union Party any more favourable tariff that it grants after the signing of this Agreement to a trade partner other than the countries of Africa and the ACP States having both a share of world trade in excess of 1.5 per cent and an industrialisation rate, measured as the ratio of manufacturing value added to Gross Domestic Product (GDP), in excess of 10 per cent in the year preceding the entry into force of the preferential agreement referred to in this paragraph. If the preferential agreement is signed with a group of countries acting individually, collectively or through a free trade agreement, this threshold relating to the share of world trade shall be 2 per cent*".

But, since we know now that the WA EPA is unlikely to ever be signed, Article 17 of CI and Ghana's iEPAs does not exclude African and ACP countries, reduces the share of world trade achieved by the partner country and does not mention a minimum industrialisation rate for this partner: "*In this Article, 'major trade partner' refers to any developed country, or any country with a share in world trade greater than 1 per cent in the year preceding the entry into force of the free trade agreement mentioned in paragraph 2, or any group of countries acting individually, collectively or through a free-trade agreement with a share in world trade greater than 1,5 per cent in the year preceding the entry into force of the free-trade agreement mentioned in paragraph 2*".

Now that CI and Ghana, alongside 11 other WA States – Burkina Faso, Cape Verde, The Gambia, Ghana, Guinea, Liberia, Mali, Mauritania, Senegal, Sierra Leone and Togo –, signed the AfCFTA[114] – only Nigeria, Benin and

[114] *The folly of the Africa's Continental Free Trade Area (CFTA)*, SOL, September 4, 2017, https://www.sol-asso.fr/wp-content/uploads/2017/10/The-folly-of-the-Africas-Continental-Free-Trade-Area-September-4-2017.pdf

Guinea Bissau did not –, they committed to opening their markets to 90% of their imports from Africa, with part of the remaining 10% being liberalised later even if it is still necessary to wait for the liberalisation scheme to be better specified, particularly with the filing of the tariff offer of each State and after ratification of the AfCFTA by 22 States, which should take at least two years.

As the partner's share of world trade is based on WTO data, Africa accounted for 2.2% of global exports in 2016 and 3.2% of world imports[115]. As a result, CI and Ghana will also have to liberalise 90% of their imports from the EU, well above the 75% forecast in their iEPAs. Especially since Article 17 of the iEPAs and Article 16 of the WA EPA do not require that "the more favourable tariff treatment" correspond to actual imports. This would imply much higher CRs losses than the already considerable losses calculated for CI and Ghana's iEPAs.

While the EU has already strongly supported the AfCFTA process[116], it has also committed to continue this support in a joint statement by the European Commission's Vice-President for Foreign Policy, Federica Mogherini, the Trade Commissioner Cecilia Malmström and the Commissioner for Development and International Cooperation, Neven Mimica: "*The adoption and signing of the AfCFTA legal instruments and the signing of the Protocol on free movement of persons are concrete commitments to liberalisation and to building on what has already been achieved at the regional level. The EU is ready to support the implementation of this impressive achievement in the spirit of the African Union-European*

[115] WTO, World trade Statistical review 2017: https://www.wto.org/english/res_e/statis_e/wts2017_e/wts17_toc_e.htm

[116] http://www.au.int/en/speeches/opening-statement-he-fatima-haram-acyl-african-union-commissioner-trade-and-industry

Union partnership and our joint political declaration of the Summit in Abidjan in November 2017"[117]. Thus, after having imposed the iEPAs, the EU will apparently win on both sides while CI and Ghana will be the fall guys!

The EU support for the AfCFTA is also in line with the European Commission's willingness to negotiate the future agreement with the ACP countries[118], which will replace the Cotonou Agreement after 2020, with the three geographical clusters of sub-Saharan Africa (SSA), the Caribbean and the Pacific and no longer with the Regional Economic Communities (RECs), of which ECOWAS.

However, Ghana has hastily ratified the AfCFTA on April 27, 2018 to increase the chances of its candidacy to lead the Secretariat of the AfCFTA responsible for its implementation, to be decided by the African Union Summit of Heads of State in July 2018[119].

Unfortunately, the other 11 WA States that have signed the AfCFTA will not be able either to tax 90% of their imports from other African countries, including from CI and Ghana even without iEPAs, since these iEPAs will disintegrate the ECOWAS CET unless ECOWAS decides to exclude them.

It is all the more absurd that, apart from CI, Ghana and Nigeria, all the other WA States are "Least Developed Countries" (LDCs) or assimiliated (Cape Verde), which will not have to liberalise their imports from the EU without a regional EPA.

---

[117] https://www.africa-eu-partnership.org/en/newsroom/all-news/africa-launches-its-continental-free-trade-area

[118] https://ec.europa.eu/europaid/recommendation-council-decision-authorising-negotiations-parnership-agreement-between-european_en

[119] https://www.tralac.org/news/article/12993-ghana-eyes-afcfta-secretariat.html

This is an absurdity amplified by the fact that the MFN clause of the regional EPA did not apply to imports from Africa and would not have required the WA States to liberalise 90% of their imports from Africa if they had not signed the AfCFTA. Incidentally, the members of the AfCFTA are the 55 African Union States and not their Regional Economic Communities (RECs), of which ECOWAS.

In other words, the damage caused to the other WA States by CI and Ghana will be much more serious than without the AfCFTA since the CDs that these other States will have to charge on their imports from these two countries will be limited to 10% and this will also be the case for their imports between them if ECOWAS does not decide to exclude CI and Ghana in order to keep the regional CET.

In this so absurd and dangerous context for all the WA states, ECOWAS should urgently convene a meeting and take the necessary decisions to save regional integration because it is in the interest of the 16 WA States to favour regional trade over that with the whole of Africa. If, according to TradeMap, WA imported from Africa in 2016 only 10.5% of its world imports and exported to Africa only 20.2% of its world exports, intra-WA imports nevertheless represented 66% of its imports from Africa and its intra-WA exports accounted for 62% of its exports to Africa.

If CI imports from Africa accounted for only 21.4% of its world imports in 2016 and its exports to Africa only 33% of its world exports, its imports from WA accounted for 75.1% of its imports from Africa and its exports to WA 59.2% of its exports to Africa. And if Ghana imports from Africa accounted for only 9% of its world imports and its exports to Africa only 24.6% of its world exports, its imports from WA accounted for 45.6% of its imports from Africa and its exports to WA 77.8% of its exports to Africa. Clearly these two countries have every interest in favouring regional integration over the mirage of a very premature continental integration.

After verifying the provisions on the MFN clause in other EPAs of the ACP countries, three regional EPAs – Cariforum (Article 19), Pacific (Article 8) and Cameroon (Article 19) – are in the same situation as the iEPAs of CI and Ghana which do not exclude the MFN clause in trade agreements with ACP countries. Given the remoteness of the Cariforum and the Pacific EPAs from the other ACP countries, this would only have an impact on Cameroon, whose rate of liberalisation of imports from the EU28-UK would rise from 79.7% in the CEMAC EPA to 90% with the AfCFTA.

On the other hand, the MFN clause will not work for the other 3 EPAs of SSA which have excluded to apply the clause in their trade agreements with the ACP countries: the EAC (East African Community, Article 15), the SADC (Article 28) and ESA (4 COMESA countries, Article 16). In addition, these three EPAs do not add the constraint of a minimal industrialisation rate for this partner that was only provided in the WA EPA.

Once again this goes to show the behavioural inconsistency of the European Commission when it systematically refuses to renegotiate the EPAs with the countries that have not yet signed them like Nigeria in WA, Tanzania in the EAC and the 5 other CEMAC States, whereas it intends at the same time to negotiate the successor agreement to Cotonou with sub-Saharan Africa as a whole, or maybe even with the whole of Africa[120].

---

[120] State of the Union speech of Jean-Claud Juncker, President of the European Commission on 12 September 2018:

It also underscores the inconsistency of the AfCFTA created to strengthen Africa's weight in world agricultural trade because the AfCFTA will have no impact on trade negotiations at the WTO until it becomes its member, as is the case for the EU which negotiates on behalf of its 28 member States. It will not particularly have bound CDs, the only ones to be negotiated at the WTO; and the future Continental Customs Union – which has not yet been negotiated – will only have applied CDs without the possibility of increasing them to the level of its own bound CDs in line with the economic situation, just as the CETs of the RECs only have applied CDs even though most member States of the African Union and RECs are already WTO members and therefore have individual bound CDs, as is the case for the 15 ECOWAS States.

Once again this advocates for the AfCFTA to be considered only as a very long-term project, the last stage of the consolidation of RECs after they have reached a high level of regional integration, including monetary and political, with in particular a large budget allocated to the less competitive States that will suffer the most from the decline in their CRs, failing which they will leave the RECs, let alone the CFTA. Following for once the example of the EU which has always devoted one-third of its budget to the Structural Funds and the Cohesion Fund for assistance to the least competitive member States such as Poland, which is the first net beneficiary of EU aid with more than € 9 bn a year, 7 times more than the PAPED for WA!

Among the many other inconsistencies and the very premature nature of the AfCFTA as described elaborately

---

https://ec.europa.eu/commission/sites/beta-political/files/soteu2018-speech_en.pdf

by Ken Ukaoha[121], let us add those from the provisions of Articles 19 and 20 on possible conflicts between the AfCFTA and the RECs' trade agreements. On the one hand, Article 19 of the AfCFTA provides that "*This Agreement shall not nullify, modify or revoke rights and obligations under preexisting trade agreements that State Parties have with third parties*", while Article 20 states that "*In the event of any inconsistency between this Agreement and any regional agreement, this Agreement shall prevail to the extent of the specific inconsistency, except as otherwise provided in this Agreement*"[122]. In other words, according to Article 19, the AfCFTA should not modify the EPAs provisions concluded with the EU, in particular those of the CI and Ghana's iEPAs to liberalise only 75% of their imports from the EU, while Article 20 states that they should liberalize 90%, given the MFN clause of the iEPAs!

[121] Ken Ukaoha, *Lessons for Africa in the CFTA before Crucifying Nigeria's President*, NANTS, April 12, 2018, https://www.thisdaylive.com/index.php/2018/04/12/cfta-lessons-for-africa-before-crucifying-nigerias-president/; *Eight Lessons on Imperatives of Private Sector-driven AfCFTA*, NANTS, April 26, 2018, https://www.thisdaylive.com/index.php/2018/04/26/eight-lessons-on-imperatives-of-private-sector-driven-afcfta/

[122] https://www.tralac.org/documents/resources/african-union/1870-agreement-establishing-the-afcfta-kigali-draft-text-march-2018-1/file.html

VIII – The EU is shooting itself in the foot by imposing EPAs

So far, the negative impacts of the WA EPA and CI and Ghana's iEPAs have been mainly highlighted for WA but they will also produce boomerang effects on the EU itself, which is shooting itself in the foot by imposing them. These effects will occur on two levels: they will increase tremendously the influx of illegal migrants that the EU does not want to welcome, and feed the terrorist movements both in WA as in the EU. They would also reduce the huge potential of medium to long term trade exports of the EU value-added products and services if the EPAs were ended.

8.1 – <u>The EPAs will blow up the influx of illegal migrants into the EU and recruitment of terrorist in WA</u>

Even though CI and Ghana's iEPAs have not yet begun to liberalise their imports from the EU28-UK, FRONTEX shows that illegal immigrants to the EU from 5 identified WA countries (Nigeria, CI, Guinea, Senegal, The Gambia) increased from 26,356 in 2014 to 91,401 in 2016[123]. The report adds: "*In 2016 more than 100,000 illegal immigrants from West Africa have been detected*".

---

[123] http://frontex.europa.eu/assets/Publications/Risk_Analysis/Annual_Risk_Analysis_2017.pdf

However, the number of migrants entering by the Central Mediterranean route would have decreased by one third in 2017, of which 52% for Nigeria (from 37,554 to 18,163) and 23% for CI (from 12,399 to 9,509). But by adding those using the Western Mediterranean route, CI migrants only dropped by 8.5% (from 14,045 to 12,854).

In fact migration to the EU remains minimal compared to intra-African and intra-WA migration. In 2017 only 17% of SSA migrants came to Europe (EU plus Norway and Switzerland) compared to 68% to other SSA countries, 6% to the US and 10% to the rest of the world[124]. Nigeria's Commissioner for Refugees, Migrants and Displaced Persons declared on 20 October 2017 that 200,346 Nigerians fled to neighbouring countries (Cameroon, Chad and Niger) in 2016 while 1.9 million people have had to move within Nigeria as a result of the Boko Haram insurgency and climate disasters.

Beyond the figures which are surely very approximate and underestimated, the real problem is that, faced with the stiffening of public opinion in the majority of the EU Member States, and the increasing assimilation made between the arrival of migrants, particularly those from Africa that nobody wants, and the terrorist attacks in the EU, the latter has reinforced the criteria for the right of asylum, forced them to return to the country of origin and dedicated an increasing part of its development aid to reducing the number of migrants arriving in the EU. This is done under cover of tackling the root causes of migration!

In fact, EU institutions, particularly France, are doing everything possible to establish the nexus between

[124] http://www.pewresearch.org/fact-tank/2018/02/28/international-migration-from-sub-saharan-africa-has-grown-dramatically-since-2010/

migrants and terrorist attacks, of which the effect is the cold shoulder given to the migrants on arrival. Thus, the Dublin-2 procedure obliges migrants to leave their fingerprints in the country of arrival on EU soil, the only country where they have to return to apply for asylum if they have meanwhile move to another EU country. In March 2018, the European Commission announced a tightening of visa for countries that are reluctant to repatriate their rejected asylum seekers and pledged another €3 bn to Turkey for retaining immigrants aspiring to join the EU.

The French National Assembly adopted at first reading on 22 April 2018 the draft law "*For a controlled immigration, an effective right of asylum and a successful integration*", which hardens the conditions for the right of asylum, notably in shortening by half the time to introduce an asylum application (from 6 to 3 months) and the deadline for lodging an appeal against an unsuccessful application (from 1 month to 15 days) followed by a systematic repatriation to the country of origin (if they have not absconded).

In his lecture at the Collège de France on 5 April 2018 for the inauguration of the Chair "Migrations and societies", François Héran pointed out that this French law deals with immigration "*with a single compass: the acceptability of measures by the public, in other words a policy based on public opinion*" [125], an undemocratic policy for a country claiming to be the fatherland of human rights. He quoted Jean-Jacques Rousseau for whom "*Domination itself is servile when it depends on public opinion, because you depend on the prejudices of*

[125] https://www.college-de-france.fr/site/francois-heran/inaugural-lecture-2018-04-05-18h00.htm

those whom you govern through prejudices"[126]. With 262,000 migrants arriving in France in 2017, or 0.4% of the population, France ranks only 16th in the EU28 in receiving migrants in relation to the percentage of the population. Guillaume Duval observes that "*France is, for many years now, one of the developed countries that receive the least number of immigrants and one of those where the share of immigrants in the population is the lowest... The immigrants pose indeed all the less concerns to the host countries, especially in the area of social dumping as they do not stay there illegally are condemned to moonlighting*"[127].

According to the call for a radical change in migration policy in France launched on 15 June 2017 by more than 300 organisations, "*The repressive management of international migration and the non-respect of the right of asylum that prevails in most countries of Europe, and in France in particular, are an appalling failure, first of all because wars, human rights violations, growing inequalities and climatic disasters throw an incompressible number of people on the roads of exile, and no police in the world will ever be able to stop young people from building a future, or families from wanting to protect their children*"[128]. It should be noted that the French associations dealing with the reception of migrants do a remarkable job and testify that beyond the attitude of the government preferring to maintain alarmist or even

[126] Emile or Education, 1762

[127] Guillaume Duval, "*L'immigration est-elle réellement une charge pour les pays d'accueil?*", Alternatives economics, mars 2018.

[128] https://blogs.mediapart.fr/les-invites-de-mediapart/blog/150617/un-appel-un-changement-radical-de-politique-migratoire-en-france

xenophobic opinions, the silent majority of the French people are ready to welcome more migrants.

Among the main financial resources mobilised for the "European Agenda on Migration" are the "EU Emergency Trust Fund for Africa" and the "European Sustainable Development Fund" as part of "External Investment Plan". But the Commission stresses that the funding promised by the Member States is not yet available.

An ECDPM study highlights that "*A recurrent issue in development finance is related to the (perceived) high risk for investment projects in subSaharan Africa that is faced by private investors but also local, national, regional and international (development) banks and financing institutions*" [129]. This study presents the EU Foreign Investment Plan to create a strong leverage to attract private investment: "*The European Fund for Sustainable Development (EFSD)... an additional new €1.5 billion guarantee which aims at leveraging €44 billion of investments through IFIs [International Financial Institutions] and DFIs [Development Finance Institutions], with a particular focus on European DFIs, to diversify the range of actors as well as increase and foster coordination and competition among them*".

Indeed the guarantees of the Foreign Investment Plan cover the whole range of possible risks: commercial risks (default of payment), political risk (coup d'état, expropriation), exchange risk, climate risks. And the Joint Declaration of the 6th EU-Africa Business Forum of 27 November 2017 in Abidjan (two days before the EU-African Union Heads of State Summit) is driving the point by calling for a "good political environment": "*The business sector is ready to scale up and facilitate*

[129] http://ecdpm.org/wp-content/uploads/ECDPM-2018-BN-101-What-Is-The-European-External-Action-Plan-EIP-Really-About.pdf

investment in critical areas, support productivity and competitiveness to create prosperity, if the right policy environment is in place. We look forward to an improved climate for investment by both European and African investors, which will also contribute to progress in achieving the SDGs. Agriculture and manufacturing should be among the priority sectors for viable business initiatives and for creating more and better jobs. European and African business organisations and companies are keen to encourage public policy measures to facilitate investment flows that contribute to sustained economic growth"[130].

The main objective of DG DEVCO (Development and Cooperation) as well as DG AGRI of the European Commission is to support the agrobusiness 'private sector' of 'modern' farms and agro-industries. That does not reflect the reality and needs of sub-Saharan farmers, of whom over 90% are small family farmers. This would not increase total production, especially for local markets, would not create the 18 million annual jobs needed and would be detrimental to the environment.

Far from tackling the root causes of undesired migrations to the EU this strategy is more likely to increase them. Especially since recent data on EU development aid do not lead to optimism. The percentage of bilateral development assistance from Western OECD countries to sub-Saharan Africa (SSA) declined from 30.8% in 2005-06 to 22.8% in 2015-16[131]. It fell for all European institutions, including the Member States, from

---

[130] https://www.euafrica-businessforum.com/sites/default/files/6th-eu-africa-business-forum-joint-business-declaration-abidjan.pdf

[131] http://www.oecd.org/dac/financing-sustainable-development/development-finance-data/statisticsonresourceflowstodevelopingcountries.htm

36.2% to 25%, while the one going to Europe – Turkey (16.6%, particularly to manage the flow of immigrants), Ukraine, countries of the former Yugoslavia – increased from 12.9% to 29%. For France, the percentage going to SSA decreased from 54.2% to 31%, for Germany from 35.3% to 11.7% and for the United Kingdom from 52.4% to 30.8%.

The three main sources of EU assistance to SSA, including WA, are the EDF (European Development Fund, financed directly by the Member States), the Development Cooperation Instrument (DCI) of the EU Budget, and EIB (European Development Bank) loans, which are also the three sources financing the PAPED (EPA Assistance Program). The European Commission has published in 2017 impact assessments of the 11th EDF and DCI. It recognises that, "*Compared to the 10th EDF, the programming of the 11th EDF has been more influenced by the priorities of Brussels and less by the choices of local partners. In spite of wide consultation, the influence of stakeholders has decreased… Responding to emerging priorities of the EU agenda has fallen on the Trust Fund (TF) for Africa, mainly financed from the EDF reserves, but its modalities risk undermining the fundamental EDF principles of partnership and effectiveness... There is a tension between what the EDF was designed to do and what it is expected to do today – with the EDF being asked to deliver on several other EU agendas (in particular security and migration) which are overriding the development agenda. The EDF11 has accommodated some of these new priorities, but there is a real threat that EDF will be pushed into responding to agendas that distance it from its primary objective of poverty alleviation... Partnership principles have been less well applied in EDF11 than in EDF10, sector and modality choices having been directed from Brussels and no further progress has been made on widening partnership to other non-state actors such as cooperatives, political parties, religious leaders, trade unions*"[132].

As for the DCI, the evaluation recognises that "*DCI has remained essentially an instrument that reflects a traditional donor-recipient relationship, and its political and operational foundations have been weakened by a number of recent developments such as... shrinking aid budgets... increasing resistance to models of development stressing democracy and human rights... Including gender equality... a reduced voice for civil society, and the rising importance of EU internal policy agendas (as reflected in the field of security and migration)*" [133].

It goes without saying that with the EPAs and the AfCFTA, the number of migrants as well as the number of people drowning in the Mediterranean would rocket more and for longer than the recent exodus of Syrians, Iraqis, Afghans and Libyans, given the demographic explosion expected in SSA and especially in WA. Without a larger EU hospitality, the surge of unemployment, misery and lack of long-term prospects would not prevent the young deprived of a future to join terrorist groups like Boko Aram in Nigeria and other jihadist movements like ACMI and Ansar Eddine in Northern Mali.

---

[132] https://ec.europa.eu/europeaid/evaluation-du-11eme-fonds-europeen-de-developpement-fed-rapport-provisoire_fr

[133] https://ec.europa.eu/europeaid/sites/devco/files/dci-final-report-vol-i-main-report_en.pdf

8.2 – The EPAs will reduce the huge opportunities for EU exports of value-added products and services in the medium and long term

EPAs are also a major threat to the medium and long-term growth of the EU because, by imposing an immediate straitjacket on the possibilities for the countries of SSA and especially WA, to start by ensuring their food sovereignty and the protection of their fledgling industries as the EU has done for many decades – and as it continues to do for its staple foods: cereals, sugar, dairy, meat and eggs – their impoverishment will deprive the EU of the possibilities to export the high-value products and services they will need in the medium and long run. It should not be forgotten that, if the EU28 population is expected to stagnate from 2018 to 2050, that of SSA would be multiplied by 2.06 and that of WA by 2.12, thus exceeding that of the EU28 by January 2030. And, with Brexit, the WA population will be 1.9 times higher than that of the EU28-UK in 1950 and that of the whole SSA 5.1 times higher.

To free themselves from the multiple constraints that the EU has imposed on their development, of which the EPAs are only one component, SSA countries, particularly those from WA, will distance themselves from the EU and develop more economic and political links with emerging countries such as India and China, and the United States, which do not impose on them the same constraints of reciprocal trade agreements.

CONCLUSION

After Nigeria's definitive refusal to sign the WA EPA the EU has its back against the wall, entangled in the very negative unintended consequences for WA as for itself of having imposed the implementation of the iEPAs of Côte d'Ivoire and Ghana while supporting at the same time the AfCFTA.

For WA this will result in regional disintegration which will at the same time make the construction of the AfCFTA impossible in the long run. Moreover, this regional disintegration of WA will penalise Côte d'Ivoire and Ghana the most, which will lose their competitiveness on their main outlet constituted by the other WA States to which they will have to pay significant CDs, while losing in competitiveness and customs revenues due to the liberalisation of their imports from the EU28-UK. They will even lose competitiveness in their exports to the EU in view of the erosion of their preferences linked to the proliferation of bilateral or plurilateral free trade agreements concluded by the EU with countries exporting the same type of products.

In the face of these future disasters, which it prefers to ignore, the EU's claim to fight the roots of unwanted migration is clearly doomed to failure as it is built on three pillars: the EPA support program (PAPED) which might shrink without EPAs; increased funds to try to reduce the flow of immigrants and to send them back to Africa; broad guarantees to private investors to modernise SSA industry and regional agriculture on the European model.

Had these fraudulent EU practices been known to the ACP States, they would not have signed and ratified regional EPAs and iEPAs, but would have asked for a waiver from the WTO to reintroduce preferential agreements as the United States did with renewed AGOA in 2015 until 2025, or to benefit from the EU's GSP+ tariff regime since they meet the criteria. And the European Parliament and Council of Ministers would surely not have followed the European Commission on EPAs and iEPAs.

But it is not too late for even Côte d'Ivoire and Ghana to reconsider their decisions, largely due to the European Commission's behaviour that misled them in many ways and its failure to honour its commitments. Article 49 of the Vienna Convention on the Law of Treaties states that "*If a State has been induced to conclude a treaty by the fraudulent conduct of another State which negotiated it, the State may invoke fraud to invalidate its consent to be bound by the treaty*"[134]. Similarly, article 1130 of the French Civil Code stipulates that "*error, fraud and violence vitiate consent when they are of such a nature that, without them, one of the parties would not have contracted or contracted on substantially different terms and their decisive nature is assessed in the light of the persons and circumstances in which the consent was given*"[135].

Rather than calling upon the bilateral mediator provided for by the WA EPA or iEPAs texts, ECOWAS and the EAC and their civil societies as well as those of the EU should resort to the EU Ombudsman, the EU Court of Justice, the EU Court of Auditors and the European Court of Human Rights, but also to the ECOWAS Court of

---

[134] http://legal.un.org/ilc/texts/instruments/english/conventions/1_1_1969.pdf

[135] https://iej.univ-paris1.fr/openaccess/reforme-contrats/titre3/stitre1/chap2/sect2/ssect1/para2-vices-consentement/

Justice[136] and the EAC Court of Justice[137] to declare null and void the signatures of these EPAs, extorted through the fraudulent manoeuvres of the European Commission.

However, beyond these possible legal remedies, the European institutions must understand that they will lose all political credibility by preventing ACP countries from reaching the Sustainable Development Goals (SDGs) by 2030 signed in New York in September 2015 and those on climate change signed in Paris in December 2015, given that, even without the EPAs, this would already be very difficult. On the other hand, the termination of the already implemented EPAs, including the interim EPAs of Côte d'Ivoire and Ghana, is a prerequisite if the EU wants to negotiate under conditions acceptable to SSA, notably WA, the cooperation agreement which will succeed that of Cotonou from 2021.

Once this EPA constraint is lifted, the development strategy that WA should implement would be as follows. Since farmers represent a large majority of the population and the food deficit must be reduced, farmers must be guaranteed remunerative and stable prices through effective import protection through variable levies[138]. Unfortunately, all African institutions, sharing the dominant neo-liberal discourse as seen with the AfCFTA and the draft CCU (Continental Customs Union), refuse to evoke an increase in import protection and find their salvation in the recourse, not very credible, to increased funding from 'partner' countries and the 'private sector'. They forget that farmers

---

[136] http://www.courtecowas.org/site2012/index.php?lang=en

[137] http://eacj.org/

[138] Jacques Berthelot, *Réguler les prix agricoles*, L'Harmattan, 2013, pages 117-153. The English version (*How to regulate agricultural prices*) may be downloaded at https://www.sol-asso.fr/articles-de-2013/

could self-finance the increase in their production if they have stable and remunerative prices and are immune from the dumping from 'partners'.

It would be desirable that the RECs (Regional Economic Communities), of which ECOWAS, become full WTO Members, like the EU, since their common external tariffs have only applied duties that they cannot raise depending on the economic situation, since they do not have bound duties which can only be negotiated at the WTO[139]. Once a WTO Member, like the EU negotiating on behalf of its 28 member States, ECOWAS will convert its bound agricultural duties into variable levies as long as their ad valorem equivalent does not exceed their bound levels.

In order for poor WA consumers to be able to sustain the gradual increase in food prices without leading to mass riots, a broad-based food assistance program, such as those of India and the United States, will be needed, through vouchers to purchase regional food products at very low prices in approved stores. This will require funding through international cooperation, including very long-term loans at very low interest rates from IDA, a World Bank subsidiary.

However this will require that the EU should stop aligning itself with the United States, which has again refused to change the WTO rules on public stockholdings for food security purposes at the December 2017 WTO Ministerial Conference in Buenos Aires[140].

---

[139] Bound duties are the maximum level that applied duties could reach, which gives a large leeway to WTO members to modify their level according to the economic circumstances.

[140] *SOL's comments on Alan Matthews' evaluation of the EU-Brazil proposal on public stockholding*, SOL, 29 July 2017: https://www.sol-asso.fr/wp-content/uploads/2017/01/SOLs-comments-on-Alan-Matthews-evaluation-of-the-EU-and-Brazil-proposal-on-Public-Stockholding-July-29-2017-1.pdf; *Reconciling the views on a permanent solution to the issue of public stockholding for food*

Acronyms

ACP: African, Caribbean, Pacific
AfCFTA: African Continental Free Trade Agreement
AfDB: African Development Bank
AGOA: African Growth Opportunity Act
AoA: Agreement on Agriculture
AVE: ad valorem equivalent
AWU: agricultural worker unit
BPS: basic payment scheme
CD: customs duty
CEMAC: Economic and Monetary Community of Central Africa
CET: common external tariff
CETA: Comprehensive Economic and Trade Agreement between Canada and the EU
CGEM: computable general equilibrium model
CI: Côte d'Ivoire
CIF: costs, insurance, freight
COPs: cereals, oilseed meals and pulses
CR: custom revenue (includes CD and VAT on imports)
DCI: Development Cooperation Instrument
DEVCO: Development and Cooperation
DFQF: duty free-quota free
DFIs: Development Finance Institutions
DG: Directorate General
EAC: Eastern Africa Community
EBA: Everything But Arms
EC: European Commission
ECOWAS: Economic Organisation of West African States
EDF: European Development Fund
EIB: European Investment Bank

---

security purposes, SOL, 22 September 2017, https://www.sol-asso.fr/wp-content/uploads/2017/10/Reconciling-the-views-on-a-permanent-solution-to-the-isssue-of-public-stockholding-for-food-security-purposes-1.pdf

EPA: Economic Partnership Agreement
EU: European Union
FFMP: fat-filled milk powder
FOB: free on board
FTA: free trade agreement
GATT: General Agreement on Tariffs and Trade
GDP: gross domestic product
GSP: generalised system of preferences
GTAP: Global Trade Analysis Project
HS: harmonised system
iEPA: interim EPA
IFIs: International Financial Institutions
INTA: International Committee of the European Parliament
ITUC: International Confederation of Trade Unions
LDC: least developed country
MAR: Market Access Regulation
MFN: most favoured nation
NGO: non governmental organisation
PAPED: EPA Assistance Program
REC: regional economic community
RO: rule of origin
RoW: rest of the world
SDGs: Sustainable Development Goals
SITC: Standard International Trade Classification
SOL: Alternatives agroécologiques et solidaires
SPS: single payment scheme
SPT: Supplementary Protection Tax
SSA: sub-Saharan Africa
TAFTA: Transatlantic Free Trade Agreement
TL: tariff line
UK: United Kingdom
UNEP: United Nations Environment Program
USAID: U.S. Agency for International Development
VAT: value added tax
WA: West Africa
WAEMU: Economic and Monetary Union of West Africa
WTO: World Trade organization

Table of contents

Structures éditoriales du groupe L'Harmattan

L'Harmattan Italie
Via degli Artisti, 15
10124 Torino
harmattan.italia@gmail.com

L'Harmattan Hongrie
Kossuth l. u. 14-16.
1053 Budapest
harmattan@harmattan.hu

L'Harmattan Sénégal
10 VDN en face Mermoz
BP 45034 Dakar-Fann
senharmattan@gmail.com

L'Harmattan Cameroun
TSINGA/FECAFOOT
BP 11486 Yaoundé
inkoukam@gmail.com

L'Harmattan Burkina Faso
Achille Somé – tengnule@hotmail.fr

L'Harmattan Guinée
Almamya, rue KA 028 OKB Agency
BP 3470 Conakry
harmattanguinee@yahoo.fr

L'Harmattan RDC
185, avenue Nyangwe
Commune de Lingwala – Kinshasa
matangilamusadila@yahoo.fr

L'Harmattan Congo
67, boulevard Denis-Sassou-N'Guesso
BP 2874 Brazzaville
harmattan.congo@yahoo.fr

L'Harmattan Mali
Sirakoro-Meguetana V31
Bamako
syllaka@yahoo.fr

L'Harmattan Togo
Djidjole – Lomé
Maison Amela
face EPP BATOME
ddamela@aol.com

L'Harmattan Côte d'Ivoire
Résidence Karl – Cité des Arts
Abidjan-Cocody
03 BP 1588 Abidjan
espace_harmattan.ci@hotmail.fr

L'Harmattan Algérie
22, rue Moulay-Mohamed
31000 Oran
info2@harmattan-algerie.com

L'Harmattan Maroc
5, rue Ferrane-Kouicha, Talaâ-Elkbira
Chrableyine, Fès-Médine
30000 Fès
harmattan.maroc@gmail.com

Nos librairies en France

Librairie internationale
16, rue des Écoles – 75005 Paris
librairie.internationale@harmattan.fr
01 40 46 79 11
www.librairieharmattan.com

Librairie l'Espace Harmattan
21 bis, rue des Écoles – 75005 Paris
librairie.espace@harmattan.fr
01 43 29 49 42

Lib. sciences humaines & histoire
21, rue des Écoles – 75005 Paris
librairie.sh@harmattan.fr
01 46 34 13 71
www.librairieharmattansh.com

Lib. Méditerranée & Moyen-Orient
7, rue des Carmes – 75005 Paris
librairie.mediterranee@harmattan.fr
01 43 29 71 15

Librairie Le Lucernaire
53, rue Notre-Dame-des-Champs – 75006 Paris
librairie@lucernaire.fr
01 42 22 67 13

www.ingramcontent.com/pod-product-compliance
Lightning Source LLC
LaVergne TN
LVHW021236061026
849535LV00008B/3083